GET PACKING!
If Not Now, When?

by

*Linda
DeBlanco*

Dedication

For my beloveds
Joey, Sweet Caroline and Jon

Always in my heart,
we roam the planet together

CONTENTS

Pre-Game Confessions

Introduction

Thanks for Everything, Lord

1 Is it My Turn Yet?

2 Appetizer

3 Why on Earth?

4 What You DO NOT Need to Pack

5 Take Me Along With You

6 Attitude – How Full is Your Glass?

7 Get Smart and Get Going

8 Healthcare

9 Homelessness

10 Worst Thing That Can Happen

11 Save Up - Break Free – Get Going

12 The Boomer Advantage

13 How Long Is Long Enough

14 Living NOW!

15 Affordable Spa Living

About the Author

WARNING – DISCLAIMER
THIS BOOK COULD BE
HAZARDOUS TO YOUR HEALTH

The sea is dangerous and its storms terrible, but these obstacles have never been sufficient reason to remain ashore ... unlike the mediocre, intrepid spirits seek victory over those things that seem impossible ... it is with an iron will that they embark on the most daring of all endeavors ... to meet the shadowy future without fear and conquer the unknown.

- Ferdinand Magellan

This book is designed to provide information and inspiration on lifestyles, travel and adventure for senior citizens.

Travel can be unsafe, detrimental for your health and even life-threatening. The purpose of this book is to educate, entertain and inspire only.   The author shall have neither liability nor responsibility to any person or entity with respect to loss or damage caused, or alleged to have been caused, directly or indirectly, by the information contained in this book.

Pre-Game Confessions

The nerve of me! I wrote this book in 2008, finished it in 2010 and here we are in 2012 (the supposed end of the world) and I am finally getting it published.

And I dared to include in the title the expression, "If Not Now, When?" Well I'm a fine one to talk, aren't I?

But wait! I have excuses. First of all I was having just too damned much fun living my retirement and following my own advice to get down to the business of publishing. And believe me, publishing IS a business.

Two years ago while hanging out on an exquisite beach in Costa Rica I did what I thought was complete the book. I was having way too much fun drinking wine on a Costa Rican beach with a very international crowd of travelers, to want to self-publish – to paper, that is. I had done that in a more energetic phase of my life and was sure I didn't want that much activity to intrude on my beach parties or any other type of party I may have the good fortune to stumble upon.

On returning to the USA two things happened. First I gave due diligence my scouring the internet to track down an agent who might track down a publisher who might wish to transform my book into print. I really gave the project a good chance. But second, almost simultaneously, I discovered that book stores I had known and loved - AND counted on - were closing their doors forever. Well, color me out of touch with progress. It suddenly occurred to me that probably the dumbest thing a literary agent could do was to take on a new author just to find a publisher who would be crazy enough to commit any new author's book to paper at this point in time. We must all just face it – the world has moved away from paper and there is no turning back.

While this (to me) shocking discovery of advanced technology in the joys of reading didn't deter my enthusiasm for the concept of golden age travel, it did put me in a bit of a state of limbo for a while. During my state of limbo, most of my peers were still declaring, "But I LOVE the feel of good old fashioned BOOKS made out of paper! I like to hold onto them, turn the pages, carry them around in my purse/pocket. I'm just not about to go electronic and I never will." Many of my friends were very adamant. This took me back to the days when the movie industry declared that television was just a passing fad and that people would get tired of it in time and rush right back to movie theaters. As human beings, our resistance to change is merely a fact of life. But, of course, all the resistance in the world does not halt progress. Although it did halt mine, I must admit, for a few years.

By June of 2011, not wishing to caste away the most significant aspects of my own advice, which is to experience the joys of adventure in my senior years, I up and moved. Taking with me pretty much all that was left of my worldly material possessions – two large suitcases worth - to the little village of Panajachel on the shores of Lake Atitlan in the highlands of Guatemala. At that time I left everything I hadn't given away (pretty much everything I owned) in the trunk of my old Buick which now sits in a friend's yard under a tidy silver cover. There it will rest in a state declared by the Department of Motor Vehicles as "non-operational" - lovingly referred to by liberated people such as myself as "non-oped." This lovely state of rest for my old Buick costs me not a penny of expense for insurance or registration fees until further notice. How do I love it – especially as at this writing the cost of gas in the USA is almost $5 a gallon and I'll have no part of that thanks very much!

Since I, myself, have been guilty of not heeding my own advice of acting NOW, I thought I had best confess. I felt the need to explain my tardiness in getting published. Seems the fun I had throughout the travels I write about in this book caused me to make this drastic move to a very foreign third world country. After just over a year, I am now fully entrenched here on the shores of my beautiful, volcano-surrounded lake. I'm living happily ever after in a land where every morning I wake up to a beautiful spring day. I have found everything I could possibly want for this episode of this particular lifetime, right here by the lake in the little village of Panajachel.

Obviously, there is another book in the joy of finding my ultimate home. But in the interest of finally living this moment of NOW, I am going to move right onto the e-publishing of this book (exclusively about traveling) with more tall tales to come in later books.

Meantime, let's get packing and hit the road.

If not now, when?

Introduction

Ah, the windows of opportunity. How they crash down with a silent vengeance while we blithely stroll through life denying even their existence.

How many have crashed down on you in your very full and very busy life? The girl or guy you should have married? The house you should have bought? How about that great job that you never should have abandoned just before the long deserved promotion? It all made perfect sense at the time.

Have you ever looked back on the windows you most regret having failed to fly through, before they slammed shut on your soul?

But Father Time marches on. With luck, hard work and decent health, we make it all the way to Medicare. We might even be rewarded with a minor income called Social Security that is somehow supposed to support us in realizing the rest of our dreams. And, no doubt, by the time we retire, bunches of lingering dreams continue to dance in our heads. Maybe some old fantasies we didn't quite get to yet because we lived too fully, slept too soundly for too long until many of our dreams slipped away. Or so we may have come to believe.

Maybe you are about to retire or have recently tripped along into that magic, golden phase of your life asking – huh?

Some of us, on reaching that magic moment of entry into the Golden Years, find ourselves extremely baffled by the shock of complete freedom. Not everybody feels unprepared and surprised. But certainly some of us do.

Am I talking to you or anyone you know?

Should you, or someone you know, happen to fit into this confused club of new found freedom riders and also suffer from a touch of wanderlust, then come with me now on the adventure of a lifetime. Come with me now while the window of opportunity is still wide open and calling you to fly through it and sail away into adventure.

Of all the windows of opportunity that have slammed shut too soon, this one might be the most important yet to be encountered. As new retirees we are at a critical, even dangerously pivotal point in our lives. The greatest danger might be to NOT act.

Clearly, by the time we retire, more of life is behind us than ahead of us. That thought alone causes many seniors to fall into sometimes serious depression. But the good news is that the due diligence of getting your kids (and maybe even your grand kids) grown up and out the door is (or should be) past. For most of us our health, though maybe not perfect, is never going to be better than it is right now.

If reaching the age of retirement isn't enough of a shock, time itself has taken on a whole new style. Have you noticed that days that used to last a good, long, 24 hours, now seem only to stretch to maybe 20? And that's on a good day! And a year, formerly 12 months long (or an eternity when you were 10), is now only about 9 months worth.

Time is flying by faster than the space shuttles used to. Yet we continue imagining we are playing on the same field of time lines we strolled along in our 30s. Back when we fancied we had all the time in the world.

Let's be realistic and brutally honest just for a quick minute. We're running out of time and energy. And, given the current fiscal health of the entire planet, even those who planned well for retirement are feeling their wallets squirm like a kid on too much Halloween candy.

If this kind of conversation so early in the game is too brutally blunt and uncomfortable, better to download another e-book quick. But if you have a wish to get out the door, and don't mind a good kick in the pants to get you there, then maybe you've come to the right place.

Time to take action if, rather than depression, you are instead inclined to dance your way through the next few years of your life tangled up in fits of fun, laughter, adventure, enlightenment and joy. I do realize all that good stuff isn't everyone's idea of a good time. But in case it's of interest to you in particular, then hear again my monotonous mantra that relentlessly calls for the answer to this most important question: *If Not Now, When?*

So, if you have a taste for adventure, come with me to exotic lands, meet bold and fascinating people from familiar, unfamiliar and colorful cultures – young and old. Laugh your way through danger and when you decide to mosey on home, you can tell your stay at home friends all about it. And show them the great pictures you took with your new fangled digital camera. You'll be the neighborhood hero! The talk of the town!

Of course, it isn't impossible that somewhere out on the adventure trail some little pigmy might just shoot you with a poison dart and that's that. Or there's always that fear we are constantly bombarded with about getting blown up by terrorists. And just when you were on your way to a good time too! It could be worse. You might just fade away leaving your kin and friends without even a good story to tell their friends about Mom or Dad's untimely demise.

It's not that I'm trying to be an alarmist. Honestly. CNN, MSNBC, FOX News, etc., are doing a far better job of that than I could ever hope to do. I'm just trying to make a point of Helen Keller's quotation at the beginning of this Introduction: *"Life is either a daring adventure or nothing at all."*

You will find that I just love to quote Helen Keller because, in my opinion, it's a rare few people who could have claimed as good an excuse for not getting on with things in life as Ms. Keller. She did, however, have the advantage of patient guidance in her amazing and determined teacher. At some point early on Ms. Keller made a decision to take good advantage of her guidance. So listen up!!!!

Many of us are tempted to take off and see the world or at least think about it. But we also have enough justifiable concerns to keep us home. It's sort of like the fear of flying from which many of us suffer and I myself did for many years.

That fear of flying, from which many still suffer, persists even though it is a proven fact that we are in more danger driving on the freeway to the podiatrist's office to get our toenails clipped. It isn't safer to drive on the freeway than to fly. Everyone knows that. But it *is* more familiar. So we go for it daily. Often we even take off on multiple dangerous freeway adventures in a single day. Sometimes we venture off to the podiatrist AND the supermarket in the same day! We generally never give a second thought to the fact that life and limb are in greater danger on the freeway than they might be almost anywhere else.

On the other hand, what the hell? Live a little. Take the safer, faster, more exciting route – FLY! It's one of the best ways I know to NOT waste precious time. And precious surely is what our time is now. Precious.

Thanks for everything, Lord

Once I knew only darkness and stillness. My life was without past or future. But a little word from the fingers of another fell into my hand that clutched at emptiness and my heart leaped to the rapture of living.

- Helen Keller

Now that we know where we're going - traveling that is - let's take this journey from the top. A sort of "In the beginning," place, one might say. And, in the interest of multitasking, this section will also, conveniently, serve as the traditional "thanks y'all" part of the book.

First, I have to tell you that I was so very lucky - blessed in fact - to enter into this lifetime in January of 1942, just one month after WWII officially reached the shores of the USofA. That makes me just a tad pre-Baby Boomer generation. But, close enough for the purposes of this book.

During WWII, what with major housing issues back home in Hollywood, where I was born, and rationing and all that, the time of my arrival was a challenge for all concerned. Rich and poor alike.

Besides the challenges of the times that everyone experienced, I was further blessed with a low income beginning, middle and who knows, end too, maybe. That is, unless this book sells millions of copies which would be totally OK with me. If you enjoy it, tell your friends about it so maybe I can make a wealthier exit from this life than my lack luster entrance. I must keep in mind that it's not over until it's over. Or so they tell me.

Now why on earth, you might ask yourself, does my humble start in life matter to you, the reader? And why would I be *thanking God* for my humble beginnings?

If this is going to be a fun trip for us, you should probably get to know who I am and who I'm looking for you to be. And, since this is my "Thank you Lord," gratitude section of this book, you should probably also know why I consider my many, many impecunious years to be a huge advantage in conjuring up this message.

Isn't that a great word, "impecunious"? Pretty much NObody knows what it means, so don't feel alone. Thing is, it describes me perfectly most of the time. So here's one of the short definitions that I feel tells it best: *"Chronically short of cash."*

Of course, most people in the USofA are not *completely* without money. But many, no let's get real, most of us, just don't usually have an overabundance of the stuff. More commonly us Americans have almost enough dollars to survive and feel guilty (or downright frantic) when we go a bit overboard on spending and cut into our daily necessities budget.

Alas, God didn't jam a silver spoon into my mouth either. In fact, I've heard not that many silver spoons were actually doled out in the 40s. And, for some reason, I didn't see fit in this lifetime to become richer than Her. God that is. You will find I frequently try to give equal time to God as feminine.

If you can relate to my strange explanation of growing up "NOT" rich, then we might just have an enormously entertaining trip through the pages of this book. I feel strongly about this "impecunious" situation because I don't think I could be writing a book about traveling on a shoestring if not for all the wonderful lessons I've learned about living life *without* an excess of the almighty dollar. As they say, "What doesn't kill us makes us stronger." Or at least, as in this case, able to write a book about frugality.

One of the great things one hopefully learns by being among the "NOT" rich, is how to find value and joy in the non-material stuff of life. The alternatives to accepting "what is," in most all circumstances (not just financial), are resentment, sadness, jealousy, anger and all around unhappiness. Sometimes pushing us all the way to deep depression. Be sure to avoid those kinds of thoughts and feelings at all cost because it's very hard to have fun and be open to adventure while living in the space of those kinds of negative emotions.

My gratitude further expands to my having been willing and able to learn and become very clear about the fact that *money does not buy happiness*.

So thank you, Lord, for letting me see beyond the almighty dollar. Let's hope this writing sheds some light on that same notion for the reader as well. Because this is NOT intended to be a book for wealthy retirees trying to decide which Central American country will give them the most bang for their retirement buck and the best equity on their RE investments in said foreign lands. It's a book for my peers who are senior citizens who are not rich. It's my contribution to retiring folks who can't imagine how they will ever see the world on limited funds.

Of course, besides thanking God for Her divine intervention in starting me off on the right foot (clad in cheap shoes), so I could write this book, there are countless others to whom I owe great and endless debts of gratitude. So on with the joys of gratitude.

As I begin this book in January of 2008, I awaken each morning in the exotic paradise of San Marcos La Laguna, a beautiful little village on the shores of Lago de Atitlan in the highlands of Guatemala. I am overwhelmed with gratitude for having gotten myself here. I am grateful for having somehow mustered the courage to step outside the illusion of safety in the USofA. Somehow I am here learning more about and learning to love more and more of the planet we call home. I am here and, I must say, that it comes as a bit of a surprise to me that I *am* here.

Besides the unusual flora and fauna, I am here learning more all the time about the people I live with and love on my planet. They are my family of earthlings, the people I meet every day on this spaceship we call Earth. I want to explain a bit about the fellow travelers I've met along the way because so much of my gratitude is for them.

I'm hoping that I'll be able to communicate to you how much fun it is to continuously meet new friends with whom one might share a drink, a meal or just a few thoughts, experiences and dreams.

The message of this book is not theoretical. I did not have an idea and/or take a trip and decide to write about it. I had an idea that grew like a healthy vine in the jungle. Once the inspiration arrived, I jumped on it like Tarzan swinging in pursuit of Jane and then I "lived" the idea. I met and fell in love with kindred spirits. Fellow travelers from all corners of this beloved planet Earth.

My new friends and co-creators of this book expanded our possibilities every day. By "our," I mean yours and mine. Their senses of adventure and enthusiasm for the intended message of this writing are boundless.

When they learned about what I was up to in the creation of this book, they shared their own stories with open hearts and minds. Besides their own stories they enthusiastically shared with me their friends and acquaintances whose input they believed would make this message more powerful for you, the reader. They "put me together" with people they were sure would contribute to this message. And they were usually "right on" in the resources to which they led me.

During my research and travels I met many, many fellow travelers who, like myself, want their fellow humans (you, the reader, who they have never met) to have adventurous and fulfilling lives. They truly do want the best for you, even though they don't know you. Now isn't THAT a nice thing to know?

Truth is, at least the "truth" I choose to believe is that the average person doesn't want war (duh). The average person wants the very best that's possible for their fellow human beings – whoever and wherever they may be. Regardless of from what country or berg my new friends had wandered, I found they would go to great lengths to share their experiences hopes, ideas, dreams and most of all their love for the good of their fellow humans.

I believe it is the natural human condition for people to want to contribute in positive ways to the lives of others. No. I do not believe that. I have seen it and I have felt it – time after time. I know it beyond a shadow of a doubt. So it is my truth.

You should know that the reading audience for whom I have created this book (you) consists of my fellow Americans and most specifically those Americans they call Baby Boomers (or thereabouts), because we are an idea whose time has come. To that end, I specifically searched for input from people who are like "us." I searched in other countries for citizens of the United States who are or will be living exclusively on Social Security income or on any type of limited monthly income for the rest of their lives.

This book was co-created in concert with many, many average people who I encountered on planes, trains, buses and everywhere else I went. I found my helpers on street corners, in hostels, hotels and restaurants; in villages, churches, ashrams, retreats, beaches, forests and jungles. These bold travelers provided me with new ideas and new contacts to further this rather unusual project.

I must add here in my thank yous a group of folks I encountered who sometimes seemed the most passionately interested in this message. I think many of them might have been your children, nieces, nephews and others who are at least a generation and sometimes even two generations behind us. I was extremely baffled when I would meet people from 20 to 50 years old who couldn't stop questioning me about everything that would be in this book, with special interest in WHEN it would be available. This phenomenon puzzled me because these "kids" were already out living adventures themselves. I became very curious about what made them so anxious to get this book in their hands.

To solve this mystery I called from Guatemala to my own daughter who lives in the Sequoias in California for the answer. She knew in an instant and offered her own enlightenment. These were her exact words. "Oh mother," she said. "That one is a no-brainer. The 'kids' you meet want to give the book to their parents so their parents will take off and really live their lives while they still can. Do you think I just want you to sit around in some old folks home if you can still get out and enjoy your life?"

Maybe our kids don't really want to hang onto us for dear life as we might like to think (or maybe hope) they do. Maybe, since they have moved on and have left an empty nest, they want to see their parents fly out of that nest and have a life as well.

The many young people I came across who seemed to feel the same way as my daughter, helped me to realize the value of my message. They helped to keep me believing that this book could be very important to at least *some* senior citizens. The encouragement of the young helped me to keep believing that there were some seniors out there who might need just a little information - some assurance that the idea of taking off with a backpack late in life is not an outrageous dream but a distinct possibility and something that is, in fact, happening all the time.

What an interesting concept, I thought. Wanting your parents to cut loose and see the world. Parents who can afford it will so often send their youngsters off to travel and experience the world before they send them to start college. I suppose the theory is that once their offspring's degree is in hand the normal stuff of life might deny them the opportunity for such a life expanding experience later. These parents must know that such experiences will be highly valuable for their offspring. But almost without exception the young people I met could hardly wait for anything they could offer their elders that might encourage them, now that they have the time and freedom, to go out and get their own expanded view of the planet.

Many of the younger people I met and told about my book were not only enthusiastic about the concept but were brimming with pride and enthusiasm when as they shared tales about how their own parents are living their Golden Years to the fullest. They were so proud to report that their parents were actually "doing" what I am only proposing. It became obvious there were two groups of "yugins". Those who wished their parents would take off to parts unknown and those whose parents were already living their adventures. The bragging of the latter group included tales of a 70 year-old mother who skydives in Brazil and many stories of parents who travel to China, trek in Nepal, stay in ashrams in India, do work exchange farming in Costa Rica and sit in rice paddies in Indonesia. My young helpers shared about so many exotic adventures in which their parents wander knee deep, with packs on their backs and stalwart hearts. They helped me continue to realize that dreams of travel in the Golden Years are alive and well and being realized all over the world. The contributions of my young friends served to further fuel the fires in me that have kept the idea of this book alive over the last few years.

My profound gratitude goes out those people, young and old, who I met along my path. They so generously pushed me forward with their encouragement and shared their love and enthusiasm so I could bring this book to you.

When my contributing fellow travelers read this book they will know that Linda Lou, whose life they touched along the way, heard every word they shared. I now share with you their words, their lives, their thoughts and all that they gave me to share with you. They shared so generously with me so that we could, together, encourage you to get out and about as soon as possible.

Our only common goal is that your golden years will shine more brightly than you ever imagined possible. So get packing. If not now, when?

In addition to the above contributors, there is another group who, while not involved in the compilation of this writing, were critical in the manifestation of it into the book you now hold in your hands.

As is true for me and as I hear of most authors, at one particular point in the process of this endeavor, my enthusiasm for continuing the work of completing this book was beginning to fade into a serious muck and mire of insecurity, relative to the value of my writing. That, combined with learning of the demise of paper books, pretty much slowed me down fairly early in the game. Then, at some point as I traveled around, as if they had just trotted down from heaven, on the movie director's cue, a gang of people roared into my life like a posse from Dodge City.

During the course of some of my travels I prepared and disseminated updates of my adventures to people in my life who would, if they didn't hear from me regularly, have been fairly certain that I was a victim of either Guatemalan kidnappers or highway robbers in God knows what country. My friends imagined that these foreign hooligans would surely have relieved me of ALL my valuables, which normally consisted of about $40 worth of local currency and a passport. This larcenous act my friends sometimes imagined would come to pass just prior to my being murdered and placed in a shallow grave if, indeed, the outlaws were that conscientious to bother with a grave of any kind.

One among my group of folks back home with whom I would communicate that I was still alive, was Claudette Welker de la Torriente from my 1959 high school graduating class. Claudette somehow was tasked with the tedious job of keeping the entire John Burroughs Senior High School Class of 1959 (of Burbank, California fame), constantly connected with each other and aware of EVERYTHING – good, fun, bad and sad. Claudette was somehow personally entertained by my regular updates and asked if I would mind if she sent them to everyone in the JBHS Class of '59. I had no idea why so many people, who were, for the most part, more or less strangers to me, would have any interest in reading my nonsense. But feeling flattered at Claudette's suggestion, I told her to feel free if she saw any reason for it.

The written reports of my adventures wander over the World Wide Web to my classmates who are by now living in all four corners of the world. As a result I received, via email, a fair amount of praise, appreciation, support and encouragement to keep sending my little tales as well as their encouragement to keep working on the fantasy of one day finishing this book.   My insecure mind worked fairly diligently to minimize my classmate's approval with rationalizations such as, "They are, after all, retired, and have nothing but time to send emails to *anybody*." Or, "They are just being kind because we suffered through the same bizarre bunch of boring teachers, even more boring assemblies, dull lunches and football rallies for three long years together. So, naturally, they think we have some sort of a bond."   It would seem that I can be extremely creative when it comes to putting down my own value. Of course, I'm sure I'm the only one who does that, right?

I am embarrassed to admit that my classmate's praise and encouragement did not fully sink into my hard head until the winter of 2009 when we attended our 50th class reunion and I got to face them – one on one.

From the moment I arrived at the first of five separate events to celebrate this golden occasion, I was continuously approached with praise and encouragement from people I barely (or rarely) recalled from school. Many people that I couldn't remember at all from school admitted that they didn't remember me from the halls of learning either. I was a low key teenager, to say the least. But somehow, during the course of reading the tales of my travels, these strangers reported they truly loved and enjoyed what I considered to be just my silly stories about pretty tame adventures. Not only that, many reported that they looked forward to receiving them as one might look forward to the next episode of a favorite TV series or soap opera.

After an entire weekend of hearing similar words of appreciation from people who had, literally, come together from all over the world, I finally was forced to reach an obvious conclusion. These guys and girls clearly did not conspire, just prior to the reunion, to drown this unobtrusive former student in unwarranted flattery for no reason at all. They didn't share their support just to be nice or just because we had the same teachers or grew up in the same mild mannered town or just because they had nothing better to do.   By the end of the weekend's events I had accept that it just had to be their honest and "for real" feedback that they were sharing with me.

So here's my book. I believed them. Their support in effect forced me to finish the book a few years ago even though it didn't get published until just now. I believed them and, I believe IN them. I thank them from the bottom of my heart. I seriously suspect that, without their feedback over that long and wonderful reunion weekend back in 2009, there would be no book in your hands at this very moment.

Thank you John Burroughs Senior High School of Burbank, Class of 1959.

At times our own light goes out and is rekindled by a spark from another person. Each of us has cause to think with deep gratitude of those who have lighted the flame within us.

- Albert Schweitzer

ONE
Is it My Turn Yet?

Twenty years from now you will be more disappointed by the things that you didn't do than by the ones you did do. So throw off the bowlines. Sail away from the safe harbor. Catch the trade winds in your sails.
Explore. Dream. Discover.

- Mark Twain

Life is amazingly full to the brim with possibilities for love, learning, joy and so much fun. If you choose NOT to dive into life feet first or head first, or whatever diving style you prefer, you may never imagine or learn firsthand how truly wonderful your golden years can be. You can encounter the best stuff where you least expect it and often without spending one red cent. You just don't know what fascinations you might bump into in the smallest little villages in Guatemala or in the middle of a rice paddy in Bali. Just open your mind and your heart and know it's there for you for the taking. And it's your turn to take it.

When I was a kid my mother always chastised me by saying, "All you want to do is have fun." Her words and tone always smacked of there being something seriously wrong with me. Well, it turns out my mother was absolutely correct. It seems I never did recover from that terrible character defect of always wanting to have fun.

Now I'm old enough to dive passionately into what my dear mother berated me for as a child. But Now I'm not feeling in the least bit ashamed or guilty about it! That's because my work is done. It is, finally, my turn. And it's your turn too. So onward to unabashed fun for us oldies. We've by God earned it!

There were times I recall, in the 50s and 60s, when you could still find an intimate night spot where ordinary people who had never met in their lives could get acquainted, jam together, be entertained with their friends and strangers and nobody even needed to pay a cover charge or pay anything at all. Back then, even just walking out your front door and sitting on the porch could be such fun. Even a high school kid could go to an old fashioned coffee house. Remember those? Wonderfully dark places with chess boards all over the place, great jazz playing, expensive (for our day) coffee. Best of all not a drop of alcohol to keep us kids deprived of the great social interaction we could find there.

I'll bet you enjoy some nostalgia about those days too. Like warm summer nights in those great old jalopies that were fully equipped with bench seats so you could cozy up to your date all evening while you cruised the main drag of your hometown, hunting for your friends who were always pretty easy to find. And when you found them, what earth-shattering things transpired? Nothing much. Yet you gabbed about nothing for hours. So this little conversation with Mom or Dad wasn't that far fetched: "Where did you go?" "Out." "What did you do?" "Nothing." But wasn't it fun?

Back then, for 30 cents a gallon, a guy could actually afford to take his sweetie for a spin, treat her to a burger and maybe even a drive-in movie. All this fun even when he only made a dollar an hour. In those days, when summer rolled around, we had no choice but to experience the warm night air blowing through the open jalopy windows. Who even knew such a thing as air conditioning would sneak into our lives to frost up our otherwise cozy dates, forcing us to begin the ongoing and apparently never ending process of shutting ourselves in. In my opinion, A/C in cars and bucket seats totally messed up the fun of summer dates.

26

Remember when we just showed up for the simple joy of people hanging out together and wallowing in the happy possibilities. Those kinds of experiences and places still exist in some of the most inexpensive and fascinating spots on Earth and it's time for us to go experience them while the going is good.

In the twenty first century, in our safe and predictable lives in the USofA, with our TV sets, air conditioning, drug commercials and the 6 o'clock news, we try to get a real sense of the boundaries of our possibilities as senior citizens. But it grows harder and harder every day to truly be comfortable in our own home towns. The more "information" (all of it a bit dubious) that we're fed the scarier the entire world appears to be. Maybe we know too much. Or maybe we just believe too much. Or maybe we have become too willing to be shut-ins.

As we approach retirement, if our 401Ks and portfolios are not securely stuffed and in place (if they exist at all), the possibilities of our boundaries can begin to appear quite grim.

To allow our possibilities to diminish as we age is to throw away America's resources (that would be us) as surely as would be the waste of a maliciously burned timberland.

We ARE the stuff America is made of. They call certain groups of us "Baby Boomers" and, for the sake of gathering together, we might as well all jump into that group even if some of us, me included, are bit ahead of that typical designation. But the term is cute, so what the hell? Let's use it.

Who we really "are," (those of us who recently retired or are just about to retire) is the cement that made our country what it is today. There may be many things about the way our country is right now that we don't like. But let's not throw away the Baby Boomers with the bath water.

We are the responsible citizens who were perhaps the last bunch of kids to get a really solid education – even at public schools. Most of us can even write in cursive without having had the benefit of private schools.

Way back in the 50s we did our homework. We did it because we knew our peers would move along to the next grade, leaving us lagging behind endlessly, if we didn't do our homework. What a brilliant and old fashioned concept! Do what you gotta do and move on. Don't do it and learn to stay behind! Not so any longer, is it?

We are the men and women who came to work on time day after day, year after year for decades. For the most part we accepted (whether we liked it or not) that the way to advance in our jobs was to excel in our own performance using our own brains, integrity, resources and energy. We realized and accepted that people who earned higher incomes had most likely earned their way to their higher positions through lots of hard work. That's how it was done, we figured.

We are the mothers and fathers who strove to be the very best parents we could be. Even in the face of the unexpected and insidious drug culture and diminishing quality of education. We strove even harder as the time came when it was no longer financially feasible for Mom to be home when the kids rolled in from school. The kids got keys instead of cupcakes and hugs. We did our very best, even when the law suddenly turned on us, demanding that we spare the rod and spoil the child.

We are the mothers, the women, who led the way in bringing respect and equality to motherhood and womanhood at a time when, if you informed

28

your employer of a pregnancy, you might just lose your job the same day. That's probably impossible to believe for today's new working mothers who instead of being shown the door "out" are instead directed to a special room to which they can retreat with their breast pumps, as needed. It's probably impossible to believe for the new fathers who now are afforded maternity leave along with their wives who are no longer insulted and harassed for taking their own maternity leave.

We are the fathers, sons and brothers who faced and fought that war that all the world knew was wrong. Including those who are not reading this book because they gave their lives in that war and don't now have the chance to live their dreams. Including those who made it home but without all their parts, only to be spit on in their wheelchairs in the streets of their own hometowns. That's who we are. And need we even ask, "Is it my turn yet?"

The term "Baby Boomers," while it sounds real cute, seems quite a petty, demeaning and actually meaningless term for perhaps the most challenged, powerful and accomplished generations of all time.

It's time now for our reward. Yet many of us, who gave our all and did our best, but in the process failed to amass a fortune, face the bleak prospects of less than golden years.

The well heeled planners, who wisely played the stock and real estate markets at every perfect moment, are to be congratulated for their wisdom and foresight. I salute them and admire them. Sadly some of us are not among them for many, many reasons and not always reasons over which we had much control.

So should the rest of us, who also worked just as diligently, now put our tails between our legs and say, "Oh well, I just wasn't smart enough about money to end up comfortably set in my golden years so I'd better stay home."

It is for those of us who worked our butts off but didn't end up rich, that this message was inspired. It is for those among us (me included) whose dreams of travel and adventure waited patiently in the wings while we did our duties – wearing down our noses on the grindstones, paying the bills, driving the kids to the doctor, school, sports events, etc. It is for those of us who generally lived lives of due diligence. We did what were raised to do and believed with all our hearts was the right thing to do and what we were supposed to do. And it was. Yet many of those who finished their life's work now believe their funds are too sparse to realize their dreams of travel.

I compiled this book because I want us NOW to realize at least some of our dreams. I want for us to fully (or at least partially) receive our reward/s – the BIG THANK YOU that we so deserve.

There's time and money enough if one is shrewd, careful and enlightened. And I'm going to show you how just maybe you can live your dreams. And I hope to encourage you to live them. Because it IS YOUR TURN!

TWO
A Taste of Adventure

There are two ways to live your life. One is as though nothing is a miracle. The other is as though everything is a miracle.

- Albert Einstein

At the start of any delicious and satisfying meal we usually like to begin with appetizers. A little something to get our juices flowing and get us thoroughly into the mood to chow down on the important stuff of the meal. So before we start to chew on the real meat and potatoes of what this book is about, let's start with some simple samples of travel adventures to give you an idea of what's possible, even on a shoestring budget.

Here is a quick prelude before we get on to some travel adventures. A quick explanation of how I got into the travel adventure business in the first place.

At the end of 2007 (the year I retired) I was visiting my daughter, Jeri, who lives deep in the Sequoias of California. One morning during my brief visit, my car became snowed in while innocently parked right outside her cabin. The cabin where she lives is situated on several acres and get to the cabin where she lives one must travel over three miles of private road that is never plowed. While I was able to remove myself from the deep snow via her four wheel truck, my old Buick was destined to remain deep in snow from early December through Spring, when the snow would finally melt, enabling me to free my poor old Buick.

31

I was not one bit enamored with the thought of spending many long months "snowed in" or going about my life without wheels. So I decided to remove at least myself from this cold and desolate situation and, like smart old birds tend to do, head South for the winter.

Despite the deep snow there was internet in them thar hills. So after a bit of World Wide Web research I settled on a jaunt to Guatemala, where I learned I could get some Spanish lessons pretty cheaply, float around the beautiful volcanic Lake Atitlan on crude ferries and live quite frugally for a few months – until the thaw. I also discovered that just by being willing to be in the air at the apparently holy moment of midnight on New Year's Eve, I could get a dirt cheap round trip flight to Guatemala.

During my unexpected shoestring visit to Guatemala, I got in the habit of periodically sending updates of my travels and adventures to my friends and family letting them know I was still alive and well. It turned out that most recipients of my updates enjoyed them a great deal and insisted that I must include these "logs" in my book. So here are some appetizers, with very little alteration. If you find these travel possibilities to be tasty adventures, you might be a bit more ready for the meat and potatoes part of the book that follows after the appetizers.

ANTIGUA, GUATEMALA – JANUARY 1, 2008

I know it sounds impossible, but I actually made it to Guatemala, alive and well, after an uneventful but sleepless New Year's Eve night in the sky. I am now in Antigua, a quaint colonial town that is a very popular destination for foreigners and Guatemalans alike. I'm in an internet café where I just enjoyed the most fabulous meal. I trusted the waitress and with a full compliment of seriously impaired verbal communications, I even dared to eat a salad! Here's hoping the waitress and I handled all the words correctly to ensure that the veggies were, in fact, washed in agua pura (bottled water) and not the local stream.

The shuttle driver who brought me to Antigua from the Guatemala City Airport told me that there are 37 volcanoes in Guatemala. But not to worry, he added. Only 8 are active! What great information to learn on my very first day. This will help me begin my visit with not a care in the world! Nothing more than possible foreign microbes in the salad, volcanic eruptions and probably earthquakes. Is this ever going to be fun!!

It is so wonderful that people barely speak English here. This means I really have to push myself to use what little I remember of Don Holler's 8th and 9th grade Spanish classes in Burbank. At least I did pay close attention to Mr. Holler so I would be sure to get all "A" grades in his class. But that was mostly because he was such a drop dead handsome guy and all us 13 and 14 year-old nymphs were goofy over him and wanted to impress him with how clever we were.

Thanks to that junior high school crush, I'm finding I can almost hold "sort of" conversations and even laugh and learn a few details about the lives and families of some of the locals I meet. I don't feel like an idiot with what little Spanish I know because when I "attempt" to communicate with anyone, we are both trying very hard to connect and it's great fun just to take on the challenge.

The Guatemalans are sweet and wonderful people - much like the Balinese, who I adore. On the plane I met a couple from Quetzeltenango who invited me to come to their home. They don't know me from the man in the moon.

What a statement about the friendliness of Guatemalans. I just might make that visit eventually.

On arrival in Antigua, I had a bit of a problem finding an available room. The placed I had intended to stay was booked up. Surprise, surprise. It was only touted by Lonely Planet (my Bible) as the best and cheapest bet in town. But I soon found a perfect room at Posada Don Quixote which is a quick and easy walk to the center of town. My room, which even has TV, is only $13 per night. Bathroom is just a few steps down the hall. The $13 rate is a little too high for the budget I'm hoping to live within, but only by two or three dollars. I'm hopeful accommodations will be cheaper when I arrive tomorrow at the small village of San Marcos on Lake Atitlan.

My first night in Guatemala proved to be quite a good time right from the start. The power went out while I was sitting in an ice cream parlor in downtown Antigua, mindlessly chatting with a retired junior high school teacher from Inglewood, California, USA. Being the innocent American that I was on that night, I thought nothing of it. It was almost as if I fancied myself at 31 Flavors in Burbank with just the slightest thought about how they could keep the ice cream cold without power. I continued my chat until I realized it was getting dark. I suddenly awoke to the reality of my situation. There I sat in a foreign land where I didn't really speak the language, I had no clue how to get back to my hotel, didn't know how long a power outage might last in Guatemala and worst of all, I didn't even have a flashlight with me!

I was suddenly compelled to dash off down the almost completely dark street headed roughly for where I thought my hotel might be. The streets in Antigua are all cobblestone and NOTHING is flat and simple or safe to walk on. In fact, the streets would not be easy to maneuver even in bright light, a luxury no longer available to any of us. As it grew darker and darker, I walked faster and faster over the irregular cobblestones with increased urgency at every step, fueled by a touch of fear and self-recrimination for being so unconscious about my potentially precarious situation. I soon enough realized that in no time there would be no street lights or any light at all to see by. Not even lights coming from the store windows would be available and a full moon was not expected.

By some miracle I made it back to Posada Don Quixote safe and sound. There I found the staff and a few guests hanging around the lobby, apparently wondering what to do next.

As soon as I reached the lobby and felt safe for a moment, I very briefly contemplated going after my flashlight and venturing back out into the streets. I didn't want to miss one night – and my first night at that – of exploration in this new and exciting country. As I opened the lobby door I thought to myself, "why not?" But the instant I stuck my head out the front door of the Posada Don Quixote the urge immediately left me. Every doorway in Antigua is set back at least a couple of feet from the sidewalks. It's just the style of the architecture there. I suddenly imagined that at least every other doorway housed a desperate, mysterious thug who would jump out, knock me over the head and steal whatever they might find. Although I seldom carry much money, I have heard that passports are great loot for crooks anywhere in the world and mine rarely leaves my person when I'm in a strange land. It would have been easy enough to relieve me of mine even though it's always kept in a money belt under my clothes. This would not likely have been a problem for the thugs since I was clearly doomed to be knocked unconscious if I ventured into the streets. My decision to remain in the dark at Posada Don Quixote was a fairly simple one.

Having quickly abandoned the wild idea of venturing out into the dark cobblestone streets, armed with nothing but a flashlight, I somehow made it to my room and got my hands on my precious flashlight. I remembered that I had brought a battery operated CD player and small but powerful speakers. It seemed the stress of darkness might be eased a bit with music. Also I remembered that my friend Jackie who drove with me to the airport had sent me off with plastic bags full of snacks. She was concerned that I might starve to death in what, to her, and most of my friends no doubt, probably seemed like the primitive land of Guatemala where NOTHING was safe to eat. So with my trusty flashlight, which had suddenly become my best friend, finally in hand, I headed downstairs to bring my little party to the lobby.

The staff had a few candles cooking around the otherwise pitch black dark lobby. I found some bowls in the kitchen and served spicy Chex snacks for everyone to enjoy. I blasted the CD player with some Gypsy Kings and everyone seemed to feel much happier and more comfortable once we got the party underway.

Obviously the party was a much safer, saner bet than passing so many dangerous doorways in the streets and it turned out to be a lovely evening with a good time being had by all. For that entire night that I was in Antigua, there was never a single flicker of electricity.

Before the world had gone dark in Antigua, I had scheduled a shuttle to pick me up at the crack of dawn to begin my journey to San Marcos on Lake Atitlan. Before leaving the USofA, I had decided to spend most of my visit to Guatemala in San Marcos. This tiny village is an unusual spiritual community where one can meditate in a large pyramid shaped temple, do yoga, get free massages at massage schools, live in a pyramid shaped cabin and learn about healing flowers and the strange and mystical benefits of chocolate. Definitely my kind of place.

SAN MARCOS LA LAGUNA, GUATEMALA – JANUARY 2, 2008

It's me again from Guatemala. Forgive the sometimes missing punctuation in these messages from Guatemala. They have very foreign keyboards here. Who would expect to encounter Spanish speaking keyboards in a Spanish speaking country? Duh. I didn't think about such a possibility. I can't find the simplest characters most of the time. Like where is the "at" (@) symbol and how does one express a question mark that is not upside down? But I'm sure I'll get the hang of it eventually.

What a wonderful challenge getting myself to San Marcos. The shuttle I scheduled in Antigua brought me to Lake Atitlan for peanuts. Can't remember the exact fare but I do recall it was a bargain for a shoestring traveler. Their usual routine is to bring passengers from Antigua to the largest village on the lake which is called Panajachel, fondly referred to by just about everyone as "Pana." From there one takes a ferry to any of a number of small villages around the lake.

I had explained to the shuttle driver that I wanted to take a ferry and to please bring me to where the ferries leave. Too bad that before the shuttle driver left I was not aware there are two locations to catch ferries, depending on which village on the lake you are headed for.

On disembarking from the shuttle from Antigua, I was approached by a few young men offering me tuk tuk rides. Who ever heard of a tuk tuk anyway? Never seen a single tuk tuk in Burbank. Feeling like the dumb American who was about to be fleeced by the local taxi drivers, I declined their invitations. I waved them off as I stood next to my TWO heavy suitcases,

37

trying to be cool and act like I knew what the hell I was doing and exactly where I was going. "Oh no thanks," I said confidently to the tuk tuk drivers. "I'm fine. I can just walk." In my confusion I forget they would have no clue what I had just said in English. Yes, dumb is the optimum word here.

When the shuttle driver from Antigua dropped me off, he had pointed to a place on the beach where a number of boats were lined up. Since I figured I was, indeed, where I needed to be, the approach of the taxis must have just been a scam to fleece the dumb tourists. I asked several people in my "sort of" Spanish exactly where I would catch the ferry to San Marcos. One would point in one direction and I followed his instructions stumbling along with one suitcase on my back and dragging the other (on wheels) over a crude stone promenade which was just up the hill from the beach. Then, wondering if I would ever arrive at the appropriate ferry, I asked again for guidance and was aimed in the opposite direction. I blindly shuffled off back to where I started, assuming the first guy just didn't understand what I had asked.

Finally, after dragging myself and my luggage back and forth a couple of times over the fairly flat but quite bumpy promenade, I realized that the pier where I really needed to be, though clearly visible, was quite a ways down the beach. I took off again with what turned out to be a totally erroneous notion – not about direction this time but about the route I planned to take. I decided that the shortest distance between two points was a straight line. Ha! I couldn't have been more wrong in this case. I headed straight for the beach, wondering how difficult it could be to get myself to the right pier to catch "my" ferry. From the edge of the water, I could easily see where I needed to go. Unfortunately it was sort of like a scenario where, from the harbor at Long Beach, you can see Santa Catalina Island only twenty three miles away. But getting there is another matter entirely.

Dumb American traveler that I admittedly was that day, I lugged my heavy bags over impossible terrain. Cursing and wondering what good a taxi would do me and still believing there was some financial wisdom in taking the beach route, ON FOOT! I trekked over sand, up and down small cliffs, over boulders and through places where having wheels on one of my suitcases was almost as useful as having wings on an elephant. All the while repeating to myself, "This can't possibly be the way this is done!"

I finally made it to the proper ferry that I needed in order to reach my destination. This after maybe an hour of huffing, puffing, literally throwing my heavy suitcases over and then scaling great mounds of boulders and wondering if there was any way I could possibly survive the folly I had signed up for on this particular excursion to Guatemala – just to avoid snow. Snow was beginning to seem like not such a bad idea after all.

At last I found my way to the right ferry and boarded for my next exciting adventure which turned out to be almost an hour bumping along on a lake that seemed instead like an ocean of wind and whitecaps. Along the way I learned from English speakers in the ferry that it was the extreme winds (the same ones making the white caps on the lake) that had caused the power failure in not only Antigua but also all the villages on Lake Atitlan and throughout much (or was it most) of Guatemala as well. Can I pick the perfect timing for adventure or what?

In my entire life, previous to this madness, I had always likened a "ferry" to the kind of affair one took, say, from Seattle, Washington to Victoria, BC. A huge white affair, grand enough to be filled with cars, buses, trucks AND people and even a mode of transportation where one could find clean restrooms and a snack bar. Maybe even a cocktail! What a surprise to find that a "ferry" on Lake Atitlan, Guatemala is merely a rickety, mostly open boat that's less than 40 feet long. It is, thank God, equipped with a crude cover for shade and protection when the large waves hit the side. The rustic seating consists of maybe 8 or 10 planks of wood nailed from port to starboard. Over time while on the lake I learned that life preservers are scarce to non-existent. Aside from the obviously foolhardy people who use these ferries, the typical cargo consists of sacks of fruit, coffee, potatoes; more sacks of mysterious unidentifiable stuff, maybe some tires and lots of other miscellaneous shopping.

[Post adventure author's note.] Looking back on the misadventures of getting myself from Pana to San Marcos on my second day in Guatemala makes me want to laugh myself silly. Much like George Carlin's suggestion that we should laugh until we gasp for breath. It makes me want to laugh in hindsight because not a single tuk tuk (taxi) driver I have ever encountered during visits to Pana or being a full-time resident for over a year would <u>ever</u> have pulled any kind of scam. At least not around the lake. My experience after spending quite a while in these parts is that the indigenous people who live around Lake Atitlan are decent, honest, helpful, compassionate and loving. Also my misadventure makes me feel so completely dumb because once I came to know the layout of Pana, it was merely simple logic that taking a tuk tuk from one pier to the other was faster (less than 4 minutes), safer and easier than dragging one's self and luggage along the beach, through and over the cliffs and boulders. And, the cost for the tuk tuk ride is LESS than one US dollar! One more post-adventure note (a few years after my innocent folly back in 2008). There is no longer a

beach. The water in the lake has risen to the extent that the beach is no more.

January 3, 2008. I am having way too much fun for a great grandmother. I didn't even get to tell you about the first earthquake, yesterday, and we have already had our second one, just this morning at breakfast. The first was during dinner on my first night in San Marcos. At least for the first exciting shaking, people got up and headed for the door. I thought about getting under the table as they taught us to do at grammar school in Burbank. But the entire thrilling moment was over before I could even decide. For this morning's episode, there was no roof to fall on us as we were on the patio where breakfast is served at my hotel. I guess meals here in Guatemala are earth-shattering experiences. For our breakfast earthquake we all just sat there, looking at each other and holding onto the tables, waiting to see what might happen next. Then everybody just laughed nervously and I'm thinking we all felt closer for having been through the experience together.

One guy who has been living here for quite a while says the lake actually softens the movement when the earth shakes here. There are no piles of rubble anywhere that might leave clues that things fall apart when these apparently frequent earthquakes happen. So I guess it's relatively safe here or at least as safe, or safer, than Southern California. But that doesn't say much, really, does it?

The fun thing is that being here, as opposed to being in Southern California, reminds me that all of life is dangerous and uncertain and isn't it better to go down in a blaze of adventure and fun than not!? So I guess I will just have as much fun as I can to the bitter, quaking end.

I am pretty settled in by now in San Marcos. I have a room here that I adore. I'm staying at a hotel called Aaculaax (pronounced aa-coo-lash). This hotel was constructed by some very creative people. There's lots of stained glass stuff around with bunches of everyday objects sort of fitted in here and there - sometimes it seems almost randomly and sometimes very intentionally and artistically. I learned that the hotel was constructed by various out-of-the-box artisans who would come to Aaculaax, do their artistic thing in exchange for a stay in a most unusual place and then move on.

My room is fabulous. It's right over the restaurant where we rocked and rolled for breakfast this morning. The restaurant is just the most wonderful patio with a great view of a huge volcano. Walls don't seem to be necessary here most of the time for restaurants since the weather is perfect almost always. Roofs do come in handy as the rainy season is a certainty for a few months every year.

The walls of my hotel are mostly filled with plastic bottles stuffed with plastic bags. No kidding. Talk about recycling. They make a framework and stick these bag filled bottles in it. Cover all that with chicken wire and then plaster over the whole thing. Lo and behold lightweight walls that won't kill you if they fall on you yet provide substance and insulation from heat, wind and cold. Imagine what the Building Permit people in California would have to say about that!

Above the four windows in my room, which I can open, there is a stained glass masterpiece across the entire pyramid facing end of my room. In the morning I can lie in bed and watch the lights, colors and shadows change as the sun comes up and I gaze at my volcano – all without lifting my head off my pillow. Not to worry. Remember, only 8 of the volcanoes here are active and they don't seem to be in my neighborhood. I think.

Many people, me included, feel that we are on an island here in San Marcos because one typically gets to this village by boat rather than by car. There are no cars anywhere although there is one road that goes around the lake. But the road does not seem to get much use. The road is used by mostly just the occasional passerby who is traveling around the lake. There isn't really a center of town in San Marcos. In fact, there isn't a village at this particular "village" at all. There are just a lot of dirt and stone pathways on which the pedestrian traffic does sometimes get dense. For example, one does occasionally have to move off to the side of the walking path so a few people can pass. That's how narrow some of the paths are.

The whole of San Marcos reminds me of when we were kids and there were these things called "empty lots" around Burbank. Anybody remember them? We would build little forts and dig holes and make subterranean houses and set up 1stores in them. It´s kind of like that here. Makes me feel like a kid again! Then there´s this fabulous place, like a grand resort (compared with the rest of the "village") where there is an internet room and a delicious café with a bar where I am right now. It´s called the Blind Lemon. It´s so elegant and modern and unlike the rest of the neighborhood, which is fairly funky. At the moment the chickens are crowing right outside the door of this lovely internet café. I love it!

The first two days I was here in San Marcos there was no power, so no internet (I couldn't write to you) and no hot shower where I stayed the first night. Most of the showers here in Guatemala (in the villages anyway) are like Mr. Coffee machines. No hot water heater but a contraption the water goes through and gets hot immediately before it comes out of the shower head. Not sure why but they call them "suicide showers." Hummm. Probably should find out before I take too many of them. At my home here at Aaculaax they have a real hot water heater that I think uses gas to heat the water because it made hot water even without electricity. But my first shower there was by candle light and I had to keep calling to the staff as the water is hot one minute and cold the next. Inconvenient but not impossible to manage as the people who can fix the problem are within yelling distance. The good news is my vocabulary is expanding. Now I know two new words in Spanish. Hot and cold! Caliente y frio!

As of today there is only one place in San Marcos to prepare and send emails. With any luck there might be two tomorrow as the other is down for a part. I talked to Christian who runs the other place. He´s from Switzerland and married to a Guatemalan woman. He says he LIKES earthquakes and believes in reincarnation. What do you think? Have I come to the right place? Plenty "woo woo" folks for me!

To get money I have to take a boat ride over the wind swept, white capped lake that seems more like the ocean during an almost perfect storm. There's no ATM at my new home town and nobody wants traveler's checks around here either. So much for careful planning. The boat rides are sometimes a bit scary. On one ride I took to Panajachel, the biggest town on the lake, there was hardly even a tiny ledge on the inside of the boat to step to while boarding. And the water was really rough when I boarded. I'm not sure how I managed to get in.at all! A miracle I think. The very bumpy boat ride was an hour to get to where I could use my ATM card and I wondered the whole way how I was going to get back out of the boat since the water got even more choppy the closer we got to our destination.

Of course, people are just wonderful here and everybody is always willing to help pull an old lady out of a boat. On return from that trip they kept putting more and more and more people into the boat. About 8 times more people than they had life preservers. The boat was listing badly to the starboard and some of us touristy types were tempted to skip the whole thing – especially me! But there was no chance of disembarking as it was a hectic and noisy affair. When I declared with some degree of anxiety that I wanted to take another boat and attempted to communicate my wish, the people running the ferry didn't and/or didn't understand.

You can tell that in the end we returned safely to San Marcos because, through one more miracle, I lived to tell about it! During this particular day of adventure, I met two wonderful ladies, one of whom I've had a few very pleasant meals with over the last couple of days. Mindless friendly chatter is easy to pull off when one is filled with anxiety.

The food here is WAY too good. It's also pretty cheap. The other night I had a gourmet meal of chicken curry, rice and fabulous vegetables with homemade bread. Twice as much a one person could or should eat and a beer. The entire bill, including tip, was about $7.00 US.

My fabulous volcano-view room runs me a whopping $11.40 per night. But I hear I might find a house for $200 a month or less. Keeping my ears and eyes open, although I honestly do love it here at Aaculaax.

SAN MARCOS LA LAGUNA, GUATEMAMA – JANUARY 6, 2008

First let me tell you that the rumors have been substantiated. I am, in fact, sleeping with scorpions and large spiders. The little black thing I saw running across my bed the other day that I prayed was a lizard, is indeed a scorpion. I wish I could say WAS a scorpion but I'm sure the little fellow is still lurking about. Helmut, the manager of my hotel only speaks Spanish and a bit of English (no German). He assures me that the scorpion's bite will not kill me. So unless Helmut is telling lies to keep guests from vacating, continue to look for updates periodically.

I've been asked several times by the folks back home about the weather here in paradise. So here's the scoop. It is not hot here. Unless you sit in full on sun and then your skin would burn. But the temperature still is not hot. However, it is also not cold. Yes, it seems impossible to me too and I have never experienced it except on rare spring days in California. Few of the restaurants have walls. Mostly just open on the sides or windows as big as almost the entire wall. I guess it's never expected to actually get cold. Some restaurants may have one or two walls and most don't have any at all - just something for shade or nothing at all. The Japanese restaurant, for example, is just a few tables out in Seiko's back yard. Fabulous food – even some sushi - and I can only talk with the Japanese proprietor in Spanish as she only speaks Spanish and Japanese. So this sweet Japanese lady is helping me learn Spanish.

Today it's mostly cloudy so it's less warm than cool but it isn't cold. You just don't see people going around sweating or fanning themselves or shivering. Maybe that means the weather is perfect. Of course, by some inexplicable miracle, I happen to have picked the three most perfect months to be in Guatemala. I'm told that one wants to be elsewhere when the rains come in May. So there you have it! The weather report.

A bit more that's interesting about where I live, other than the joy of sleeping with scorpions. It seems my hotel is mostly constructed out of trash. As I explained before, the walls are made of plastic bottles stuffed tightly with plastic bags all jammed together in a rough frame and then chicken wired and plastered over. There is a wall around a school nearby where they have left the bottles exposed in certain areas so that people can get an idea of how this is done. It seems very brilliant to me, especially in a place with such temperate weather and where there are earthquakes. Having a wall of plastic bottles and bags fall on you couldn't be as bad as a wall of bricks and mortar.

I learned that they didn't have any idea when they started building my hotel what it would turn out to be when it was done. In time, it just happened to turned into a hotel. Lots of volunteers worked on it and it's unclear so far exactly why they bothered to start in the first place – since they didn't know where they were going with the whole idea. I learned that my room was sometimes used as the bar as it's right by the restaurant. One whole wall in my room was clearly intended to be a bar as there are wood sections that can be completely removed above a narrow bar-like affair along the bottom of that wall. I'm thinking of having a birthday party, removing the wood sections from my room and serving drinks for all my new friends. I've already gathered a whole bunch of new friends. Actually I've gathered almost too many new friends to keep up with even though in truth I don't have a thing in the world to do here!

It's hard to believe how much is always going on around here in San Marcos, although it seems so amazingly remote, quiet and peaceful. For example, the last three days have ended in parties, parties, parties. First it was the DVD party at Hotel Quetzal where a heated discussion followed the movie about the Mayan calendar in all its 26,000 year cycles – same number of years for the Hindu cycles. hmmmmm. After that discussion a bunch of us went up the road to a pizza party at a strange place that I think is actually a restaurant. They have two very unique ovens there with seating all around them. These ovens are fashioned in clay in the shape of the heads of birds. I think the fire happens in their mouths. It's supposed to be

47

very symbolic. California Pizza Kitchen would have killed to produce such good pizza for a whopping $7 each. People sang, played guitars, smoked a bit of pot, drank beer and, once again, a wonderful time was had by all.

The next night we met at a restaurant where we were supposed to have a discussion for people who wanted to make plans to go to a Rainbow Gathering in Cuernavaca, Mexico. Apparently this Rainbow Gathering is a bunch of hippies who get together to oooh and aaaah and call each other sister and brother for days on end. I don't know if the "rainbow" part is anything like what "rainbow" signifies in California. The entire rainbow affair sounded like a bar at midnight to me. An entire bunch of hippies here in San Marcos had originally intended to plan a caravan to go meet up with another bunch of hippies already arrived in Cuernavaca, Mexico for the big event. But unfortunately the first group had set up their camp right next to three rivers. Seems it rained and the whole little rainbow community, including gear, supplies, horses, people and all, had washed away leaving that good idea literally up a creek. So the discussion of taking off for Cuernavaca to meet the other hippies transformed. We instead got into a circle (I guess San Marcos is a gather in a circle kind of place). This guy Miguel went through twenty Mayan affirmations complete with everybody waving their hands in the air to express as many "we are connected to the earth – we are one – we are way cool" concepts as we possibly could in the time originally intended to plan what turned out to be the ill-fated hippie gathering in Cuernavaca.

Then last night there was this huge party at Blind Lemon, the unlikely restaurant and internet café up on the one and only actual street around here. That started at 8 p.m. But first a bunch of people met at Patrick's house at 7 p.m. For a name changing party. Well dudes name used to be Patrick until last night. We all stood around (in a circle, of course) in the

48

former Patrick's current back yard. We formed a big circle and talked about what we wanted our new name to be and why. I went to the party for curiosity since I was OK with my name. But after I listened to the whole thing I decided that, yes, I would like a slightly altered name. I guess I figured, what the heck, when in San Marcos do as the woo woos do. My choice of a new handle was not elegant or romantic like some of the others who chose new names like Estrella (star), Lilly Lucia and Mamish. One woman did choose "Barbara," however. I chose to be called Linda Lou (sounds like I'm from Alabama) because that's what Carol, my dear friend for half a century who I went all through high school with, always used to call me. Way back to 14 years old.

A little side not, speaking of Carol. My take on retirement is that it is THE BIG THANK YOU that we get when we've worked for half a century and finally get to live our lives just for ourselves. My dear friend Carol, however, passed away on November 18, 2007, just a couple of months before I got to Guatemala January 1, 2008. In my eyes, Carol was cheated. Her passing before ever even getting to enjoy one day of retirement or enjoy spending one social security check, was one of the reason I feel this book is so important. We all should get at least some portion of a shot at that BIG THANK YOU. And life being what it is, we probably ought to get to that reward a fast as we can. Like how about NOW!

As soon as I declared my new name, everyone started calling Linda Lou. Every time they do – which is often as this is a very tight little community - I feel somehow like Carol is along with me for the ride on this grand adventure. Now I introduce myself as Linda Lou to the many people I meet and I decided last night to dedicate my book to Carol who I always called Sweet Caroline.

49

After the name changing circle, most people strolled up to the Blind Lemon (combo restaurant, phone booth and internet café) where I was astonished to discover we had a professional jazz singer from the San Fernando Valley, California who was absolutely magnificent. She was accompanied by equally talented jazz pianists. All this fabulous entertainment totally out in the middle of nowhere in a place that rocks and rolls even without music. This had to be the happiest, liveliest, most unpretentious, joyful party I have ever been to in my life. It was so cool (the party – of course not the temperature). The whole scene actually brought tears to my eyes. Before long the tables got pushed to the sides and everyone, myself included, was dancing around madly. No one seemed drunk or high. We were just completely happy and prancing more than dancing, with no inhibitions whatsoever.

There's a wonderful lady here who everyone calls Tooth Fairy. She is missing a tooth or two right in front. Tooth fairy, who is from the UsofA, looks like she may have just rolled in on a shopping cart from the streets of Santa Barbara – a prime location for street people. She was here a year ago when a Guatemalan woman had a baby but the mother died right after childbirth. Tooth Fairy says this baby adopted *her* and she has been here ever since, toting this beautiful one year-old orphan in a large leopard patterned scarf, Guatemalan style. Tooth Fairy attends simply all the social events. I first met her at the pizza party a couple of nights ago. She spent last night dancing around Blind Lemon for the whole time I was there (until almost midnight) with this beautiful little Guatemalan baby girl tied to her body.

Except for sleeping with scorpions, things have been a bit dull around here. No earthquakes lately. One of my friends pointed out that an earthquake could also be referred to as earth dancing. I like that. I'll keep that in mind and instead of freaking out for the next earthquake I'll just remind myself that the earth is dancing again. I love being in a neighborhood where some of the potentially most frightening events can be seen as a good time.

All those parties took place over the last couple of days. For tonight's entertainment, Il Forno, an Italian Restaurant down the path, is showing Sicko, the latest Michael Moore flick. So I shall end for now with more to come in the coming days.

SAN MARCOS LA LAGUNA, GUATEMALA – JANUARY 14, 2008

Things have been quite peaceful here in Guatemala lately. A small boulder did crash to the ground yesterday at my favorite restaurant, Moon Fish, which has the most beautiful view of the lake. But, I was prudent. I moved to the other side of the restaurant so I was a few feet away from the potential boulder crashing area. Just in case. One never knows.

I hadn't previously noticed but many buildings around the lake are built right into the rocks. For example, Helmut (the manager of my hotel) took me on a tour of the Honeymoon Suite today. You can see a lot about my hotel if you go to www.aaculaax.com. Copy that web address into your browser and check it out if you get a chance. Much of the walls of the honeymoon suite are simply the boulder that the whole place is stuck to. My room (far from boulders) is the best, of course, but the ones you can see on the website are pretty nice too, although they cost a few Quetzals more than my $11.40 US a night. But $85 is not too shabby for a two story honeymoon suite with a kitchen, living room, bedroom, surround sound and outdoor bathroom with spectacular views of the lake throughout the entire suite. It's a gorgeous place with fabulous stained glass windows everywhere. Only downside is that in the event of an earthquake, the place has great potential to either fall hundreds of feet off the boulder it's built on or be crushed by higher up boulders. This extra version of rock and roll must add a little excitement to the beginning of a new marriage.

There seems to be a temptation here in San Marcos to build things right smack next to the boulders that are just hanging around the lake. They build things up so high that it makes one dizzy how many stairs one must climb to get to the really good rooms. The builders of Aaculaax must not have considered for a second the possibility of earthquakes sending the whole damned honeymoon suite tumbling hundreds of feet down the cliff s. What could they have been smoking? Well around here that's a silly question. It's kind of like us out of the box humans get big kicks out of living on the edge of danger – particular around here. And HERE I am so what kind of out of the box character does that make me?

Today there was a chocolate class at Paco Real. How many of those have you been invited to lately? The teacher is this old guy, Keith, who looks like he greatly regrets the end of the hippie era. Keith places himself in the middle of a large, round, shaded area that amounts to a sort of huge palapa. The structure is just a frame to hold a roof that's made out of a whole bunch of palm leaves. I suppose this must in function be like the conference center at a Hyatt, but enormously different in architecture.

All us hippies, young and old, sit in a big circle (there's that gather in a circle thing again), like theater-in-the round, and listen as if Keith really had something HUGELY IMPORTANT to tell us about chocolate. I've never been terribly fond of chocolate and Keith wanted money so I left before he passed the hat and then passed out the samples. Later that afternoon I saw some of the paying customers who stayed for the entire class. They were amazed at how "high" they had gotten drinking Keith's chocolate concoctions. Seems after he gave people his concoction he then led a meditation and people were crying and getting quite goofy. Imagine! Hours later they reported they were still feeling high. Keith had roasted the chocolate before preparing it for his students. Roasting is a very important part of the process, apparently.

At breakfast this morning (shortly after the boulder fell at Moon Fish and before the chocolate class) I met Ron who lives way up on the hill just on the outskirts of San Marcos. Ron claims he taught Keith everything he knows about chocolate. Ron further claims that if you roast chocolate it loses most of its fabulous qualities, nutrients and drug-like effects. Keith, silly boy, does roast his chocolate. These people around here must be really desperate for entertainment if they can spend that much time and energy on CHOCOLATE and its consciousness altering effects!

I am getting very excited about my book lately. The more I get into it, the more I get into it. I am continually meeting young people - several times a day. Everyone around here asks a million question. Not much else to do. Why are you here? What are you doing here? Why Guatemala and not some other country? Why San Marcos and not some other village? How long are you staying? Where did you come from? Where are you going? So eventually I get around to telling them that I'm going to be here for weeks - maybe months - and that I'm writing a book. Of course, they insist on knowing what it's all about. These yungins get so excited that they are asking me to send them, via email, even the drafts of what I've written so far. Seems they almost urgently want to pass this revolutionary information on to their parents to encourage them to get off their retired duffs and hit the road. I don't think it's about rushing their inheritance - do you? Although there is that potential, I suppose.

This morning I had a flood of ideas for a chapter on becoming intentionally homeless. I believe this is a great solution for people on limited incomes to follow my golden years travel strategy. I got so excited about intentional homelessness that I just couldn't stop writing. By hand. Now I have to get busy and type up all that I wrote this morning. So this is the end of this Guatemalan update.

SAN MARCOS LA LAGUNA, GUATEMALA – JANUARY 18, 2008
Well yesterday, I couldn't imagine how I might share some Guatemalan excitement for today, January 18th, in honor of my 66th birthday. I wondered where I could muster something exciting to write to you about because life here in San Marcos has settled down to such an amazingly peaceful, wonderful existence. And aren't we all looking for more excitement than that? Well some excitement came my way and here goes the tale of this very special birthday.

The morning started out looking almost like the real world in that I had to set my alarm clock! Heaven forbid! This travesty because I had to wake up early so I would have time to have breakfast before my very first Spanish class at 9 a.m. with Estella, my new Spanish teacher. I saved a bit of time getting ready to face the day because I didn't have to wash my face. This little task was not possible this morning because there was no running water at Hotel Acculaax. The water in San Marcos apparently fails to come to work until a little later in the morning.

Despite that one little time saver, I was still in a "hurry up" mode when I dressed and left my room. I rushed off to my restaurant patio before the coffee had even finished perking and ordered breakfast. Imagining that I am in a tropical country (as it often appears to really BE a jungle out there – no kidding), I put on pants to the knee and sandals as I do every morning.

As on this particular morning I was out the door a bit earlier than usual, I hadn't realized it was still a bit chilly and my legs and feet were getting cold on the patio as I awaited my coffee and breakfast. So I thought I would just run quickly into my room and put on at least some long jeans.

I believe I shared with you in an earlier message that I had run into a little black scorpion on my bed on my second day here in San Marcos. Since meeting my little black friend, who I affectionately call Amigo Negrito (little black friend), I have been very cautious about putting on clothes. I always bang my shoes together in case he has chosen one of them for his new great room. I always shake out – with vigor – any piece of clothing I put on.

Oh, but how easily we can become complacent in paradise. In the two weeks I've been here I hadn't shaken Amigo Negrito out of a single shoe or blouse or even seen any trace of him at all since the second day of my stay at Aaculaax. So this morning I quickly ran into my room, pulled off my short pants and pulled on my jeans. For the first time, I failed to shake them. In two seconds I immediately realized what had happened. Amigo Negrito had taken a powerful chomp out of the most tender part of my leg, the soft skin on the back of my knee. I have never removed my pantelones with such gusto and fear and not to mention speed. I was in complete disbelief. My brain wanted me to believe I was just being paranoid – it just couldn't be! But from the feeling on the tender place behind my knee I was certain it was NOT an ant or even a spider that had just had its way with my precious skin. And I was sure it was certainly not my imagination!

In a split second the jeans I had just donned were removed and I began to shake them with great enthusiasm, all the while continuing to hope my imagination had simply gotten the best of me.

55

But no. My little Amigo Negrito appeared on the floor in all his maybe 2 ½ inches of pitch black glory. Pretty little critter, actually.

Amigo Negrito made no effort whatsoever to flee. He may have become stunned and perhaps he was even poisoned, having just partaken of the blood of a Californian.

Seizing the opportunity and moving faster than a senior citizen has the right to move, I massacred the little creep with one fatal blow from my favorite sandal.

One doesn't need to spend too much time with Buddhists, which I had just done within the last few months, to suffer instant and extreme remorse for such a brutal act of cold-blooded murder.

Immediately following the brutal act, I turned over my sandal to be sure I had really eliminated the little creep. Unfortunately I immediately began to feel regret and deep concern for my karma.

I quickly pondered what my options had been, trying to excuse my murderous behavior with the flimsy justification that sleeping with Amigo Negrito these past two weeks had not been my favorite part of this adventure up to today, my birthday of all days. Of course, logic prevailed and the knowledge that his cousins (there are an awful lot of cousins in Guatemala), brothers, nieces and even worse his perhaps over-protective parents were surely still lurking and living quite comfortably in my room - somewhere.

I quickly apply Campho Phenique to kill any subsequent pain from the sting, after apologizing to his beautiful tail, all that was left of the corpse of my assailant. From there I went directly to my patio and announced to

Tina, the restaurant manager, that a scorpion had just attempted to have me for breakfast, before I had even gotten my delicious coffee. Tina, a beautiful German girl, was not at all certain what to suggest except to propose that I might not want coffee as it could stimulate my blood. That was her only suggestion, just in case scorpion venom was now flowing through my veins. Well, Tina didn't use those words (about the venom) but only suggested not partaking of the coffee – just in case. My vivid imagination made up the rest and added the venomous part.

Leonardo, another breakfast regular on my patio, was also present. He didn't say a word, which is normal behavior for Leonardo anyway. When Tina left I asked him what he thought about the incident. His only answer was that he had never heard of any bad outcome in San Marcos from a scorpion bite or sting. But I was a bit concerned with his input thinking that perhaps Leonardo not only doesn't speak much but perhaps he also doesn't listen either. Then, much to my shock, Leonardo got on his cell phone (of his own volition) and called immediately to Cindy, our neighborhood holistic healer and the only person in San Marcos with any type of medical expertise at all. On completion of his call Leonardo passed on Cindy's medical wisdom that generally people have no problems with San Marcos scorpion stings, other than some pain and/or itching.

Based on Leonardo's report I decided a morning without coffee simply wasn't worth the sacrifice, even if I was going to be the one and only exception to the positive prognosis for scorpion bites in San Marcos. So I enjoyed my huge, delicious cup of Guatemalan coffee, downed my breakfast and went to my first Spanish lesson at 9 a.m., straight up. It is now almost 5 in the afternoon and I am still alive to tell the tale. I guess holistic Cindy knows her stuff!

I decided to look at all the benefits of having gone through the "bite" experience on that very special birthday morning.

First, hopeless Polly Anna that I am, I was glad to have the fear of getting stung by a Guatemalan scorpion over and done with. It's now behind me and I didn't die. Praise the Lord and pass the coffee.

Next, it was probably a blessing from God for my birthday. I really like this one. No doubt I have now become invincible – protected in all my adventures so I can complete my book and make a positive difference in some senior citizen's lives.

Also, I can honestly share, from my own personal experience, that the sting of a scorpion is not necessarily the end of the life as we know it.

Lastly, going to sleep with scorpions each night will/should be much more relaxed having put this fear behind me. That is, if I don't become obsessed with the revenge of the familia de Amigo Negrito.

All of these far-fetched benefits only further prove that when life gives you lemons you can, indeed, make lemonade. Here in Guatemala they make it with mint and soda water. It's fabulous and very, very green.

Moving right along to subjects less fascinating than scorpions.

Today I had my first Spanish lesson here in Guatemala. My teacher, Estella, will be coming each weekday to San Marcos on a ten minute ferry ride from San Pedro. She can only work in the mornings because her three children are out of school by afternoon. I have signed up for 2 hours of lessons, Monday through Friday, from 10 a.m. to noon for a cost of about $43 per week. Estella comes to my hotel where we meet in the gorgeous garden in the middle of Hotel Aaculaax. We sit for my studies at a built-in table, the top of which is a work of art made of hundreds of pieces of glass and tiles. The table is made of junk, no doubt, as that is the building material of choice that is used for the entire work of art called Aaculaax, my home these days.

I had no idea it would be so much fun learning Spanish in a one on one format. My two years in junior high school Spanish, where I was in love with Mr. Holler the teacher, are coming back to me. I am thrilled at the thought that someday I might actually be able to hold a conversation in a foreign language.

There are two people in San Marcos at the moment, Gabriela and Angel (pronounced Anhell) who claim they are from Mexico. Personally, I don't believe it. I believe they are from some other planet. Angel plays an instrument called a "hang" (sounds more like hong) that looks exactly like a flying saucer, to me. He says it was invented in Switzerland about five years ago but I think he brought it from his planet – and I don't mean planet Earth. The hang (pronounced hong) definitely has an "other worldly" sound. Gabriela plays a small harp and they wander from restaurant to restaurant playing and singing for tips and apparently working their way through the country. Gabriela sings in some unidentifiable language – also probably from their planet – and in a voice that is definitely not of this world. Mexico! Ha! They can't fool me!

Gabriela and Angel have told me where they plan to be playing tonight and I think for my birthday I will just follow them around and drink scotch wherever they go. Happy birthday to me.

I've taken to drinking straight scotch on the rocks (rocks made of agua pura), if I drink any alcohol at all. If I do have alcohol, I never have more than two. Drinking scotch instead of wine is my choice because one glass of wine here costs about two dollars as does a bottle of Two Buck Chuck from Trader Joe's in the USA. I can't handle the comparison – moneywise, even though that same glass of wine in a restaurant in my country might be as much as $8.00, US. On the other hand, scotch on the rocks here costs less than $3 and I couldn't get such a deal in a bar in the USofA. Well, except in a couple of fun dives I know about or maybe at the American Legion but then I'd need a sponsor just to get served. It's all about my views on spending money (always wanting more bang for my buck). It really has nothing to do with which drink I prefer. Psycho!!!!

I must reiterate that I am careful not to drink too much here. Not only because I am so cheap and regularly impecunious but also because the paths I must tread to return to Aaculaax after an evening out are rich with obstacles. Pretty much every path has the most uneven surfaces imaginable. Every step is pregnant with the opportunity to crash and land in a two foot deep gutter or a least on my duff or with my nose in dirt.

And then there are the dogs. Oh, the dogs. Better be fully conscious on the chance of an encounter with one/some of them. People have told me sometimes the dogs act like a pack of wolves at night and seem to want to bite. This has NOT been my experience as they all seem overly friendly, harmless and even lethargic to me. Sometimes one dog might look a little agitated but I just talk to them like you might talk to a two year old baby and they wag their tails enthusiastically. However, just in case I am wrong and "they" (those who fear the dogs) are right, I want to be sure to have my wits about me when it's pitch black dark out. What if I have to kick some chow in the chops in the middle of the night, when I'm all alone, and the batteries on my flashlight have died, and I can't see a thing, and I'm far from Aaculaax? At the very least I want to be SOBER! Don't worry. It's perfectly safe here – usually.

A couple of days ago I went to Panajachel (Pana to us locals) which is about an hour away by ferry. I needed to get money from an ATM or bank and a few other necessities not available in San Marcos. There I met Lynette to whom I had been referred as one of several Canadian and American women, close to my age, who have come to call Guatemala "home". I lunched with Lynette and Judith (both from Canada) at a sidewalk café. As luck would have it (is there really such a thing as luck) most of the other ladies I had wanted to connect with wandered by as we ate lunch and of course, being the small town Pana is, everyone knew everyone else. I now have names and telephone numbers for these very interesting people. My hope is to get to know these ladies and to add a large chunk into my book that describes what it has taken for them to leave their cushy, safe lives in civilized countries and take up residence in this particular land called Guatemala. I am hoping that their stories might inspire people from the USofA who not only want to travel but might even consider making foreign lands their homes.

I shall leave you with my birthday plans for the evening exposed, hoping you are not still reeling from the scorpion incident. I get hungry around this time of day so I must be off for now to see Gabriela and Angel and see what new adventures I can get tangled up in.

SAN MARCOS LA LAGUNA, GUATEMALA – JANUARY 28, 2008
NEWS ALERT! AMIGO NEGRITO HAS COUSINS!

61

This morning, as I opened my eyes, the sun was just poking itself over the top of one of my several volcanoes, bringing brilliant light to my lovely stained glass windows. The same thought that crosses my mind every morning presented itself, right on cue. It goes like this, "How on earth did I ever get to sleep last night."

It is, in fact, a huge puzzlement to me that I am sleeping with scorpions. They are so exotic and adorable that at this stage in my adventure sleeping with spiders around seems like mere child's play to me. For a couple of days I chose to live in the illusion that I had done away with the resident scorpion in my room at Aaculaax, which I have recently learned has a name. My room is called "Restaurant." The rooms at Aaculaax don't have numbers, they have names and since mine is right over the restaurant it is, naturally, called "Restaurant". Apparently my room is famous for scorpion sightings. It's smaller than a small town here and people who have been around for a while are very familiar with EVERYTHING that goes on in the neighborhood – down to the smallest details. When I have shared about my scorpion experiences with locals, they always seem to have their own tales of sightings in the room called "Restaurant."

Yesterday morning I was preparing to go to breakfast and have the best coffee in the world to accompany my amazing new crepe concoction on the patio right outside my room. I noticed something odd. I had placed my copy of *Life of Pi*, the novel I am reading, on a shelf right above where I sleep. The front cover was slightly raised and there was a black "blob" just on the first page of the book, just under the cover. I had just placed that book on the shelf myself the night before when I finally (and miraculously) got drowsy, so I knew this blob was some kind of creature who had arrived during the night as I slept. It didn't seem to have a shape but was just a black blob. It was definitely not a spider and I wasn't interested in examining it too closely lest it be some kind of jumping creature. Who knows in a place like this?

Since the brutal murder of Amigo Negrito, my little friend who chomped on the back of my knee on my birthday, I had lost interest in any further killings. So I quickly got a glass and put it over the black blob. I was surprised that when I looked through the glass, feeling safe enough to get a closer peek at it, I still could only make out a black blob. I wondered how a blob could have climbed into my book, so I began to move the glass back and forth, thinking that whoever was there under that glass was certainly sleeping peacefully. To my amazement the blob awoke and literally "blossomed" into the most beautiful black scorpion. The creature suddenly took shape, including the most gorgeous curly tail and precious little pinchers. It sprung into action in the most amazing way. Obviously Amigo Negrito has cousins after all.

Of course, this latest early morning encounter put to rest any illusion I might have entertained that I had successfully (albeit regrettably) exterminated "the" creature of the room called "Restaurant". Of course, my first thought was to end my residency in "Restaurant," leave Aaculaax and perhaps return to the security of the civilized comforts of the United States. Then I remembered the Interstate 5 that runs through California like a spine and other even less safe freeways and highways. I quickly recalled the cabin in the Sequoias where my car remained detained by deep snow until spring, when the thaw arrives. Only bears and mountain lions to worry about in that neighborhood. Oh yes, and freezing to death. In the book I'm reading, Life of Pi, a young man from India, who had been traveling by Japanese freighter to Canada, becomes a castaway on a lifeboat with a Bengal Tiger, who has already eaten a hyena and an orangutan. Talk about a fantastic, tall tale. Life is never really perfect, is it? It's always something. So why worry?

On realizing with the blossoming of this critter into its "awake" state that it was, indeed, one of Negrito Amigos cousins, I quickly decided that I would not be involved in any ongoing brutal murders, especially unjustifiable murders which the one on my birthday certainly had been. I feared if I were agreeable to further assassinations, that I might become a serial killer. So what if it's only bugs and stuff. Who knows where things might end if I start down that path. I further decided that, since it's always something anyway, I might as well just continue my stay in the room called "Restaurant" and make the best of my roommates. Maybe we can learn to live in harmony. At least it's worth a try.

So after an awesome breakfast of the best coffee in the world and my amazing crepe concoction, I asked Helmut, the hotel manager, to please go to my room and remove the blossomed blob to another place of residence. And I accepted that I will never know how many cousins are really living with me. I've not heard a single story of anyone in San Marcos expiring from living with these creatures so I can pretty much promise to keep you posted on these matters. I feel confident and can assure you that if I don't return to California, it will not be due to any hostility between me and my roommates.

I'd like to say a few words about the general environment here in San Marcos.

I've come to love the wind around my lake. Or, it may be more accurate to say that I've come to thrill to the wind here. It's like an exciting friend that drops by just as life has grown a bit monotonous. The sun, without the accompaniment of the wind, is tropical and burning warm on the skin. The wind, which is not warm or cold, just windy, acts only as a very strong fan would on a hot day in anyone's home town. It cools ones baking skin perfectly then stops, almost as if it knows it's done its job to perfection. That's on a normal, perfect day when we might refer to the wind as a strong breeze. The thrilling days are when you hear the telling sounds in the distance and you know its coming. I perch every morning on my veranda with perfectly balanced sunshine at my special table. I've claimed my special table because there I am provided just enough shade from the banana and papaya plants to protect my skin and just enough sun filtering through the leaves to keep me warm and cozy.

How is this for tall plants? I am on the second floor on my patio and these plants tower another twelve or fifteen feet above my head. They are tall. On a normal day, as a gentle breeze moves these plants around in a kind of seductive dance, I sit in a constant state of perfect comfort with sun and shade moving intermittently over me for at least a couple of hours each morning. This condition of ever moving sun and shade is the perfect setting for a beautiful open space filled with laughter, birds, blue sky, fluffy white clouds, splashes of plants and flowers everywhere. We are always joined by a menagerie of friendly dogs mulling about the tables and sometimes falling asleep on my feet.

Then, I hear it coming – first in the distance. There's a kind of dull but very ominous roar. I've learned there is a distinct pattern to it. Once the dull and distant roar starts, the full force of the wind always follows, arriving right in our midst. Then everything around us dances furiously as we become the center of the roar which is completely ignored by all. It almost feels that the entire magical space around me is breathing – just to prove how completely alive it is.

During my first few days here I was afraid and intimidated by the wind, fearing it might toss something right at me that could cause me some damage. My instinct was to protect myself from possible flying objects. Now I'm becoming rather addicted to the excitement that the wind brings with it. When it's really acting up it often causes the power to go out. It's just a kind of routine happening here. That may sound like a minor problem unless you find yourself on an isolated path in complete blackness with a broken flashlight or no flashlight at all. There is no way to know if or when the power will return but there are, fortunately, options. The most magnificent option is to simply stop and gaze at the stars. It's kind of fun to feel how your heart can pound just from becoming a speck of nothing while observing from blackness the amazing view of the universe as seen from the inside of a volcano – which is what some people say my lake actually is, after all.

Among other of the less wonderful options when the power fails is panic. Not my favorite so forget that one. Another, just standing still until someone wanders along who does have a flashlight and is willing to escort you home or wherever you might be going. The good news is that the person with the flashlight will probably be someone you know who is also probably headed where you, too, are headed as there are not that many places to go around here anyway.

Today is Sunday. You would not think a Sunday in paradise would be any different than any other day of the week. But it is. People here – the visitors – don't just wile away their days doing nothing. They spend their weekdays in bizarre classes with subject matter such as, "the moon" and "the sun" and sometimes they go into "silence" for days on end. And then there are the chocolate and healing flower seminars too. Remember this is a community of many former hippies and lots of "woo woo" people. The "silent" ones pass people on the path with simply a smile. On occasion the "silent" ones will put a finger to their lips indicating they are in silence and have no intention of talking with anyone. Sometimes, when they are getting bored with being in silence for days, they will hold up their hand showing one to five fingers so you will know how many more days they will not be chatting with us. Many, the lucky monied people, have regularly scheduled massages. Or they are attending massage schools. A large benefit to the impecunious here, such as myself, is that we can volunteer our bodies for practice massage sessions – for free or just the cost of the oil.

Also, a common site in San Marcos is to come across two or three people seated at small tables in jungle-like settings. They might be anywhere. In the gardens of hotels, restaurants, etc. They appear to be a part of some very serious business conferences. They are, in fact, simply engaged in Spanish classes, one on one or sometimes one on two with teachers who barely speak English or like my own teacher, don't speak English at all. With all the classes, massages and other activities that move always move at a snail's pace, it's hard to believe that a Sunday still feels very much like a Sunday anywhere – only without the NFL.

People go to Sunday brunch here in San Marcos. But it's very different. Here they bring guitars, accordions, cigarettes, dogs and, shoes are optional. Try that in California! Not a single part of the restaurant by my room called Restaurant has walls except the kitchen which is downstairs so who cares? Roosters crow through the entire delicious experience of Sunday brunch.

Seated next to me on this Sunday morning is a group of young multilingual people trying to decide what's the better mode of transportation to visit a volcano and some ancient ruins in the jungle. The big issue is should they travel via tour bus, shuttle or chicken bus. Seems a simple decision but last night at Moon Fish (one of the restaurants I frequent – also without walls) I learned that there are important things to consider in choosing transportation around here.

It seems it is less likely that one will be robbed on a chicken bus but you are more likely to lose your suitcase when it falls off the roof where it may be traveling with a number of people and possible animals as well. These are, in fact, not easy decisions.

On the other hand, on a shuttle or tour bus you may preserve your suitcase but be relieved of your passport, credit cards money and maybe clothes (to be sure you are not hiding valuables). I'm thinking I'll skip the more exotic side trips into the jungles and simply wallow in the joys of my little (tiny) village of San Marcos where I can just live quietly with my scorpions.

Yesterday I went to Panajachel on a one hour ferry ride and bought a soft piece of foam for my otherwise hard bed. Seemed a good investment for $20 since I plan to live right here in "Restaurant" for at least two more months. As I'm resolved now to "settle in," this morning I asked the owner of the hotel (pretty much in jest) if I couldn't get my room painted in a color more to my liking. Instead of laughing at me he was very concerned about what color I would most like.

Is this place strange, or what!?!?!?!

It's turning into evening here in paradise and when that happens my feet start to get a bit chilly. So I shall now head to Paco Real, the most amazing restaurant right next door to my office, Rapinet (the local internet cafe), where I type this stuff into a computer. At Paco Real (where I experienced my first Guatemalan earthquake) there is a fireplace and I can get a bowl of lentil soup and a basket of homemade bread for 20 Quetzals or just under $3.00 US. Often we have free live entertainment to go with our tasty meal. And I do especially enjoy the fireplace action!!

SAN MARCOS LA LAGUNA, GUATEMALA – JANUARY 29, 2008

Big surprise! I have to move from my lovely little room called "restaurant" in just a few days. My plan had been to stay in San Marcos for the entire duration of my three month stay in Guatemala. Oh well, "The best laid plans of mice and men oft go awry." So some famous guy told us way back when.

How fitting that I am being ousted due to previous reservations made many months ago to accommodate a writer's conference. This gathering is to be held here in San Marcos for a whole week starting on February 10th. And I don't even get to attend the conference. What an all around slam for a budding writer. The real world has pushed me to move away from the peace and serenity of San Marcos and, being a hopeless Polly Anna, I resolved to not only make the best of the situation but to somehow turn it into the most fortunate coincidence of my entire trip to Guatemala.

The mostly road-free village of San Marcos is quite small and has only a finite number of available rooms. Apparently, the fastidious writers snagged just about every reasonably priced room in the village months prior to my arrival. Since every other village on Lake Atitlan is a ferry ride away I was truly cast adrift.

Where to go next?

69

Since there are no ATMs or banks in San Marcos I had made a couple of day trips to Panajachel during which I learned that many American senior citizens have taken up full or part-time residence in that little lakeside village. As Pana is the largest village on the lake it clearly would offer me a wealth of opportunity in gathering material for this book. So I decided to spend the week of my eviction talking to some folks who are living the same dream that I am promoting in this book.

A few days in advance of my date of eviction I ferried to Pana to find a suitable and inexpensive hotel where I could spend a week doing some research and meeting lots of people.

While on my room-finding misssion to Pana my plan was to also pick up a new pair of Guatemalan pants that were being custom made just for me. What a deal. Custom made for the amazing price of $20 US. While visiting the tailor, the fickle finger of fate gave me an unexpected poke. The tailor's friend Chico was in Herrardo's shop keeping the tailor company that day. When I asked the gentlemen about cheap hotels, Chico told me (in Spanish which I was somehow able to follow) that he had an apartment available that could be rented but not daily or weekly – only on a one month basis. It came complete with TV, fireplace, bathroom, easy chairs, a darling garden, hot shower – everything including the kitchen and the kitchen sink. All this for a mere $300 US, for an entire month. Since I fell in love with the idea of a fireplace and TV, and since the overall expense for a whole month would be less than most hotels I had found up to that point, I decided to put my original plans to stay at San Marcos for three months aside and seized the opportunity to stay in the darling apartment in Pana for a full month, at least. It also happened to work out to be less than my room at Aaculaax.

I moved all my two suitcases into my new digs on February 10th, happy with the beginnings of a new and unexpected adventure in a place where I hadn't planned to spend any time at all. It was only two days later that I received the most tragic news of my life in that cozy little place.

*(**Author's note:** I have wrestled for many months about including in this book the following February 13th update which went out to all my friends on that day. Since it was a very real and very significant part of my experience during this particular trip, in the end, I decided to include it. I have opted for inclusion based on the fact that painting an entirely rosy picture of travel is unrealistic. The real world is all around us as we travel AND the life you left behind is happening as well, just as if you were right there worrying about and trying to save everyone and everything in your own little world.*

PANAJACHEL, LAKE ATITLAN, GUATEMALA – FEBRUARY 13, 2008

To my dear friends and family,

This is a very sad update. I just learned last night that my son Joe, only 41 years old, passed away in Sacramento sometime during the last few days.

As most of you know Joe suffered for many years with addictions and mental illness and was most recently receiving shock treatments at a Sacramento mental health facility. We are not yet aware of exactly what happened but when I know more I will let you know.

My close friends and people who have themselves suffered along with their mentally ill family members, will understand that the call I received last night did not come as a surprise. I have, in fact, spent many years intensely agonizing and worrying at the prospect of receiving the exact call that came last night. Today it feels very much like that agonizing worry was somehow rehearsal for the real call that I always feared would come one day.

People close to me have stood by me with so much patience and love over the years. They stood by me through what I realize so often seemed like (and often was) irrational worry, together with my endless, futile attempts to help (save) Joe. In the end I shall not continue to blame myself as I have through so much of the torment of the last 15 to 20 years. I have come to realize that there never was and never would have or could have been anything I could have done to save Joe. I want those of you who know how often I have blamed myself to know that I will not live the rest of my days feeling responsible for the tragedy of Joe's life.

Although I am, of course, devastated by this tragic news, in some strange way I was prepared. Perhaps it is much the same as with someone who has lived through a loved one being terminally ill only to ultimately lose that person, despite our worry, prayers and even futile actions. I believe, and recently went through this myself with my dear friend Carol, who passed away last November, that there is, at some point, comfort in knowing that our loved one is no longer suffering. So please know that both Joe and I are going to be fine. Joe is at last at peace. The painful worry I carried with me for so many years will, in the normal course of events, transform into grief. In working through grief, I have heard, there is a beginning, middle and end. So I am hopeful that with the help of those who I know love me, I will survive and eventually find peace.

This may seem a strange decision but it is still my intention, between tears and sadness, to continue with my mission here in Guatemala. My closest friends and family members, who I know are deeply concerned for my welfare, have encouraged me to not return to California at this time. They have assured me that what needs to be handled will be handled and that my participation in those activities is not required.

72

I don't know that I have really made it clear to all of you who are receiving this sad message, about the intention of my book. In wrestling with the decision to return home or stay here in Guatemala, what I realized in the last few hours is that my book truly is about LIFE. Life is, after all, he most precious thing we have going for us. And what is more important than using life to the fullest? I have come to believe that it would be wrong and not in anyone's best interests to abandon this mission. There is nothing I can do in California to bring Joe back to us.

My book is entitled *If Not Now, When?* There is great potential for my book to make a huge contribution to many people's lives. And, as the title implies, time is of the essence – especially when dealing with the precious gift of life.

In case you don't receive a cheerful, interesting and amusing update for a while, just know that one will be coming to you before you know it!

PANAJACHEL, LAKE ATITLAN, GUATEMALA – MARCH 12, 2008

After a month of sadness, rationalizations, adjusting, confusion, amazement and endless discoveries, I have finally reached a point where I can get my fingers once again hover over a keyboard.

In that time I have collected the most amazing assortment of wonderful new friends with whom I spend hours gabbing, doing lunch, dinner, visiting their homes, attending lectures and events, going to movies and something even more wonderful. During my moments of grief and sadness at the loss of Joe, that overtake me out of the blue, I am incredibly supported by these amazing folks. I am especially cared for by the indigenous Guatemalans who never laid eyes on me before last month. It's as if I have known them for years, not only as friends but almost as if they are members of my family.

73

The good news is I'm still living here by beautiful Lake Atitlan, basking in the glow of the most wonderful, compassionate and loving people. The bad news you already know. And despite my falling into pits of profound grief and sadness when I least expect it, I am surviving pretty well.

Here I am in the largest village on Lake Atitlan called Panajachel (pronounced Pana**h**achel and fondly referred to as "Pana"). This place is pretty wild compared to San Marcos. In San Marcos the sounds consist mainly of roosters crowing before dawn, fire crackers any old time and who knows for what reason, a bunch of very happy birds. The most unusual ear polution in San Marcos is the croaking of the girl at the church who must have bought candy with the money they gave her for her singing lessons. I think they set out to find the girl with the worse possible singing voice. Maybe to keep people awake or who knows. And finally the sometimes fairly loud swishing noises of the trees in the heavy winds that are very common around the lake at this time of year.

Some say San Marcos is not the "real world" because it is filled with spiritual seekers from all over the world who sit cross-legged and silent in a huge pyramid-shaped building looking for the meaning of life inside their heads.

People in San Marcos also complain that there are too many people in the village to speak English with so there is not the pressure to practice their Spanish as there is in other cities, towns and villages throughout Central America. However, all of that fairyland stuff worked just fine for me and in San Marcos I had my little scorpions to keep me company, if things got too serene.

Foreigners who come to a place like Panajachel are not exactly the same as people you would meet in "Anytown," U.S.A. – even though that is where they came from. For example......

One of my best friends here is Diana, a 60ish Californian who came to settle here in Pana where she has a compound consisting of several acres of beautiful flora and fauna. She has subdivided her property and plans to sell segments exclusively to healers of all types, ultimately creating a spiritual community. Diana has her own business which is conducted on her property. She is a spiritual teacher and healer. I just didn't happen to have such a thing down the street from me in California. This may sound wild to many, but Diana's business is thriving as this lake is considered to be a very spiritual area that attracts many, many people with these types of interests. In addition to one-on-one sessions she conducts group seminars on various aspects of spirituality, incorporating Christianity, Mayan principles, past life regression, angels, general all around joy and fun, etc.

At this writing, Diana and I are in Santiago, a 20 minute ferry ride across the lake. We are staying in a fabulous stone bungalow complete with fireplace, TV/VCR, coffee pot, incredible artwork everywhere, and most notable, water *you can drink* that is plumbed right into the bathroom – unheard of here as drinking water (at least for non-locals) comes only out of plastic bottles. Good news though that the bottles can transform into walls later.

We have come to Santiago for a music festival that is presented as a benefit to rebuild the hospital here which one of the serious victims of Hurricane Stan in 2005. In case I haven't mentioned it before and/or you haven't heard, that Hurricane erased one entire Atitlan lakeside village from the face of the earth, including many, many of its inhabitants and most everything else. It was deemed not particularly newsworthy apparently, because competition from Katrina in Louisiana around the same time made this catastrophe seem minor by comparison.

I have another friend, Skip, who is in Panajachel to both learn Spanish and do research to organize Guatemalan adventure packages for senior citizens who are far more on the wealthy side than my impecunious self. Skip has been leading adventure tours for 30 some years. In the beginning of his adventure career his customers were younger. But in time, his customers became senior citizens so now he leads tours that (while still full of adventure) are especially designed more for oldies. This way he gets to have the same customers to lead around jungles and such year after year but just provides them with a new and different "buzz."

Then there is Azeria (AZ he likes to be called). He is a big burly guy who looks like he would squash a Harley if he sat on one and also looks like he has sat on a few in his day. AZ comes to the lake for a few months every year just for fun, when he tires of the chilly winters in Colorado. AZ is a hoot and a regular at the bar I am currently frequenting.

In addition to bars, I frequent two internet cafes depending on time of day. In the morning and early afternoons I click away at Emilio's place on a street called Santander which is the main drag here in Pana. When Emilio (who does not speak a bit of English) learned of my son Joe's passing (as related to Emilio in my pitiful Spanish), he became my big brother and spiritual adviser. Every day when he sees me he stops whatever he is doing to make absolutely certain that I am feeling as he puts it "tranquillo" (peaceful). Although he doesn't speak English he makes his caring and compassion perfectly obvious as we stumble along with my poor Spanish and his complete lack of English.

Two days ago a fellow named Kevin was at Emilio's place while I was pounding the keyboard. Emilio so humbly and in Spanish asked me if I would help him with a negotiation with Kevin who wanted to purchase a large quantity of items for resale in the Bahamas. There was no one else around to help Emilio and I felt that I was a pretty poor candidate to handle any kind of negotiation requiring English/Spanish translation. But I decided I had better give it a try and in the end both parties were completely satisfied with the outcome and I, myself, was totally amazed. Today it is all a blur and must have been somehow a miracle as I can't recall how it could have worked out so well. I was extremely happy because, had I not been there and somehow able to help my dear friend, Emilio might have missed what could become a great opportunity for him.

This encounter also supported my belief that improving communications by teaching English to people like Emilio can greatly improve potential for non-English speaking people everywhere in the world to live better, more prosperous lives. I became all the more interested in the great benefits of possibly becoming a certified English teacher myself, as well as becoming all the more enthusiastic about promoting that concept in my book as an excellent way for seniors to work their way around the world AND make a contribution to bettering people's lives.

I have a lot more great friends here who it will be very difficult to leave when the day comes for me to return "home." Home is rather a strange concept for someone who lives happily in two suitcases. It feels very much like "home" to me, right here in Pana.

About those two suitcases, I've given that lots of thought lately and have decided that two suitcases are truly excessive. I have come to believe that two cases are actually too much of a home for me and I've decided it's time to downsize considerably.

For example, three jackets and a sweatshirt I now believe amounts to two jackets and one sweatshirt too many. One jacket would probably do the trick just fine. Three pairs of shoes is one pair more than a person with only two feet needs in Guatemala and two pairs of shoes is probably one pair more than most of the locals even own. You might be surprised at how many of the locals don't even have one pair. I have a few items of clothing with me that I have never worn. Somehow it's just like when I had a huge closet! But in this case, the burden of a second suitcase is more annoying than a large, overstuffed closet that never moves. As my mother always used to say whenever she possibly could – and in this context it seems entirely appropriate, "This is not a fashion show!"

Speaking of fashion shows I wish I could do justice to describing to you the music festival Diana and I attended in the dirt under a mix of very beautiful pine trees, banana plants and other tropical looking plants. I swear the growing things here just can't decide if they live in the mountains or the jungle as there is a proliferation of flora that seem perfectly suited to either/or/and every type of environment.

The festival was an amazing throwback to a meeting of flower children in, say, Golden Gate Park, San Francisco in the 70s. Attire consisted of an unbelievable "everything goes" as long as it was not pretentious. Although very interesting glitz was expressed throughout and modesty didn't seem to be a consideration. So that was just a joke. It was ALL very pretentious!

The aroma of cannabis filled the air (although they tell me it's illegal in Guatemala) and there was quite an amazing feeling of freedom. There was no sign of law enforcement anywhere. At one point, my friend

Diana mentioned she had just enjoyed a most delicious chocolate pastry and pointed me in the direction of where she had found it. They had run out of the delicacy she had enjoyed by the time I arrived. So I wandered off in search of chocolate. Chocolate is something I rarely, under normal circumstances, even think about but once it's mentioned the thought just refuses to leave. With chocolate on my mind, I came across an American-looking woman with a basket on her arm filled with what looked like chocolate cupcakes. I asked her what they were. Her response, "These are space cakes." I could feel my eyes almost pop out of my head with disbelief and she obviously noticed my big eyes too. I said, "Do you mean what I think you mean?" To this she replied, "They will send you into space." I don't know why exactly (or, maybe I do) but I decided not to go there. The culture shock here is enough to make one plenty high, just rubbing up against it. Probably I missed a great opportunity but color me chicken.

Yesterday my month was up and I left my apartment (fireplace, TV and all). I might have stayed longer but I needed to get away from the spot in front of the fireplace where I was standing when my friend Teri called to tell me about Joe's passing. Polly Anna that I am I decided to turn my escape from the memory of that horrible and traumatic moment into something positive. So I decided to move.

Tomorrow I start a whole new phase of my stay in Panajachel. I call it SPA LIFE. I recently signed up to use the health club at a luxury hotel. For only $25 US, I am now (and until I leave here on April 2nd) an official guest of Porto del Lago, a five story luxury hotel by the lake. In addition to using the treadmill in the beautiful health club (the treadmill had been my only interest, really) I was please and surprised to learn that I am also granted full privileges to use the gorgeous swimming pool for lounging by and swimming in, the Jacuzzis and the wonderful, large, clean showers in the dressing room where there is also a beautiful sauna. Sitting by the pool one has a glorious vista of the lake and the all the volcanoes that surround it. I'm a guest all right – I just don't have a bed at this luxury hotel.

Tomorrow I move to a room across the street from Porto del Lago where I will sleep perfectly comfortably and safely for just under $7 US per night. Rooms at Porto del Lago start around $120 per night plus tax, etc.– a bit more than I will be paying at Casa Loma for the entire month. Here in Panajachel I can eat for about three weeks on $120 U.S., without ever lifting a pot or a pan. So, all in all, I have created a very pleasant miracle for myself. For just under $8.00 per day I will live steps from the lake and spend my days exercising, sitting by the pool reading good books, writing a good book (I hope), drinking screwdrivers out of my orange soda bottle and watching the sun fall down behind the volcanoes every night.

Even if I could afford it, I would never spend $120 a night on a place to sleep, since I wouldn't be able to see what I was paying for because when I sleep my eyes are closed. And besides, look what a wonderful chapter this is going to make for my book: "Luxury Spa Living for Under $8.00 Per Day."

I was sharing this amazing spa concept with some guys at my favorite bar the other day and a senior citizen woman, who almost seemed hostile, demanded, "How can you do that!?" After I explained she said, "Well maybe. But the pool isn't heated!" I guess it's true after all. Some people just can't get past "the glass is half empty" no matter what kind of fabulous miracle you present to them. Possibly (duh) the first step in the pursuit of happiness is a sincere desire *to be* happy. Without that, all that glitters isn't even going to be noticed – whether it's gold or not.

Well, I guess I'll close for now with this final revelation. The beatniks of the 50's, the hippies of the 60's and the flower children of the 70's have not vanished from this earth. They are alive and well and living on the shores of Lake Atitlan in Guatemala in one village or another. Many actually aged, as we might expect. But just as many are amazingly still only in their 20's. The current generations must have discovered what a good time we were having.

One more miracle!

PANAJACHEL, LAKE ATITLAN, GUATEMALA, MARCH 21, 2008

Hola Amigos y Amigas,

For me, life in Guatemala becomes more worth living every day. I have this theory that travel to strange lands should be a mandatory prerequisite to graduating into life.

Because we often, in our work-lives, only travel for vacation time, we probably tend to get the impression that travel is a luxury, reserved only for special occasions. Like wearing a tuxedo.

But to me, the things we don't get to learn about the world and about ourselves when we DON'T travel are essential lessons that just should not be missed.

First, how about what I have learned about myself.

People sometimes send me messages saying that I must be brave or courageous. If you only knew how far from the truth that nice compliment is.

As I believe I have explained in previous messages, I am currently living in a village on a large lake. How ironic is this? I just noticed this morning that we can use the letters LA to describe Lake Atitlan. So I'll do that. And I must also interject that the other LA, closer to y'all in CA, is at least AS scary and maybe even scarier than it is here.

If I am brave and courageous for living at LA, then those of you who live in or around cities like the other LA – the one in California - are every bit as brave. But you just don't think about it because it seems so normal to be on a freeway and sitting on a major earthquake fault. In fact, it is probably more dangerous where you live than where I am right now.

But let me tell you more about my transportation challenges here in Guatemala.

What drew me to LA, Guatemala in the first place was a map of Lake Atitlan in the Lonely Planet guide for this fair country. In that map there are tiny dotted lines representing ferries connecting villages around the lake. In my naive mind, before I got here, a lake was just a great big puddle. A hole where water accumulated for lack of an easier route for some river to reach somewhere farther – like to get the water into an ocean. More good reason to travel – to relieve myself of such a childish notion as that one!

My puddle here at LA can be nearly as wild and unpredictable as the ocean. And I have come to respect it just as much.

On a clear day, in the morning especially, I can't imagine any greater joy than racing across the glassy, shimmering surface of Lake Atitlan, past our three beautiful volcanoes, all neatly lined up in a row, like the Great Pyramids of Giza.

Until recently I had only wandered among the small villages on the northern edge of the lake. Going from village to village along the north shore is like riding a city bus that stops every few blocks. Same drill in a LA, Guatemala ferry. Takes a while to get where you are going. But on this ride the scenery is truly beautiful. So who cares how long it takes?

Lately, however, I discovered Santiago, which is a village as far across the lake from Panajachel as you can get. The ferries to and from Santiago don't stop anywhere along the way. It's like a direct flight straight through the middle of the lake. So what does this have to do with courage you ask?

Well, it's the same lake if you are headed for Santiago or San Marcos. But an entirely different experience. On the milk run route to the other villages it becomes apparent that the waters along the shore are usually sort of calm most of the time. The captains on the milk runs are always looking for people on private docks who want to be picked up so they cruise along at a peaceful clip for the most part, so they can pick up passengers along the way.

The non-stop flight to Santiago, on the other hand, is a different matter entirely. The trip to Santiago takes less than half an hour and since there is absolutely no reason to slow down, they don't!

Besides this method of thrilling, mucho rapido (very fast) travel, the water through the middle of the lake is dramatically different than the peaceful waters of the milk run around the edges of the lake. It's like the ocean out there in the middle of the lake. It can be especially fierce on a windy day and on almost any afternoon.

So while the early morning skim along on the peaceful glassy waters is heavenly, the afternoon trip, if you want to go home (which I always do), can be absolutely harrowing.

I have, now that it's time to go home to the USA, become accustomed to Mr. Toads wild ferry ride back from Santiago.

Another challenge of life in the middle of LA, Guatemala is what my imagination can do with the prospect of capsizing out there in the lake in what feels more like the ocean than a puddle. Which is what I used to think a lake was. The milk run always stays pretty much close to the shore so I don't worry too much on that journey. Not only do I know how to swim, but also I am on the plump side. How's that for a graceful way to describe the f word – fat! So floating just comes naturally for me. Left to my own devices and even without a life preserver, I have no problem on the milk run imagining myself making it to shore if need be.

However, just when I was starting to get comfortable and confident about taking the ferries, I was reminded by some fellow American's that few of the local people here know how to swim. At all! And then there's the almost complete absence of life-preservers on board most all ferries. Many, maybe most ferries have no life-preservers at all. Three preservers perhaps for thirty five passengers is quite common.

My imagination can run wild with the idea of one of the race driver captains plowing through the middle of the lake (the middle being far, far away from the shore) and flipping the freaking ferry in his rush to have the shortest run time from Panajachel to Santiago on record.

So how's this imagined scenario for manifesting fear just so I can be brave. Ha! (The following didn't happen. - not to me anyway. It's just a wild fantasy of mine.)

I'm out in the middle of the lake, as I said. I'm far, far away from the safety of the shore. No life-preservers and a wild, record-breaking Guatemalan captain flips the boat. But suppose that instead of just breaking my neck and that's that - instead when the boat rolls over, I end up in the water uninjured and still able-bodied and bobbing like a plump buoy. Only trouble is that the other people who used to be in the boat are now in the water too and 90% of them don't know how to swim. I'm not sure I would ever even get into a boat if I didn't know how to swim. But there's no YMCA here and how else are they going to get around – what with the ferries being the routine Rapid Transit Authority of Lake Atitlan? Many, many people who live around the lake go to work in the ferries every day (my Spanish teacher for example). It's no different, I suppose, than the way we jump in our cars and get on the freeway believing we're safe. Ha! So there they are in my wild fantasy. These mostly small, spindly and skinny little Guatemalans, thrown out of the capsized boat. They are looking for anything that's floating to keep them alive. And what is still bobbing around, since my mother made sure I knew how to swim AND tread water? Me! The big, beautiful, bobbing buoy of LA. I'd always thought knowing how to swim would be enough and had never given a thought to other people wanting to use me for a life preserver.

I don't believe it is courage that moves me to climb into the ferries here. I think it's just a matter of priorities. I want to live my life as fully as possible, even more than I want to be comfortable and safe. So I board the boats - fear and all – with the optimistic idea that I'll make it to the other side of the lake unscathed, alive and well.

You know how they always tell us that statistically airplanes are safer than the freeway? Many of us, me included, still find an airplane provides a scarier experience than a freeway. It isn't usually the *actual* danger that stops us. It's more often than not just fear of the unknown – the unfamiliar. I have no more courage than anybody else. I guess I'm just left-brained enough to go with statistics even though I'm right brain enough to create the wildest and most dangerous fantasies! I have, in the last two and a half months, said so many times to myself, "Chances are you will survive." Every single time I have said that, I have also managed to survive. So I guess I'm coming to see these kinds of dangers as familiar and therefore much like the LA (California) freeways. Just getting used to them is more than half the battle.

So that was just a little blurp on overcoming fears and ferries scene. Now how about how good it might be for us to travel so we can learn to understand people in foreign lands – how they think, feel and live.

Yesterday in Santiago I was having lunch with a couple of gringo friends and my Spanish teacher who I have adopted. My Spanish teacher, Estella, understands quite a bit of English but doesn't speak much. Well, at this lunch we had this very deep conversation about life but it had to be all in Spanish. So I'll interpret for you. Ha! What a hoot THAT is!

I asked Estella why I see so many Guatemalans smiling and laughing all the time. I wondered if they tell jokes to each other all day or what is the deal?

Estella immediately answered my question by explaining, "Because they are happy." What a lesson we could learn from the poor people in a country that most of us wouldn't even consider visiting. It's not like we don't have a lot of reasons to avoid Guatemala, since most people in the US think it's deadly dangerous. I mean, you would surely be kidnapped just outside the airport doors if you even got that far. And everybody's so poor it must be too depressing to visit such a place.

Well, Guatemala is some of those things. But it is so much more that is, surprisingly, good and positive.

Guatemala has been deadly dangerous for the Guatemalans but mostly because of unrest brought on my many forces outside the country and by people who are not Guatemalans. A lot of their stresses and lots and lots of killings were, during the civil war, brought on with the support of the government of the United States of America. But I know you don't want to know about that.

Usually only rich Guatemalans are kidnapped – for money, of course. And it is true that far more people are poor and struggling than rich and comfortable. But isn't that true everywhere? The poverty at least eliminates the possibilities of kidnappings among the poor.

So why, then, with all those frightening possibilities, are more Guatemalans per capita smiling and laughing in the streets than the per capita numbers of people in my country who exhibit that kind of behavior?

Every night I walk down Santander, the main drag here in Panajachel. By the time I get home, the village is usually shut down. Guess I'm just that kind of a "party 'til they roll up the streets" girl. Along my walk I notice that the heavy metal doors are mostly closed over the many, many stores and restaurants. In places along Santander where there is not a store there is usually a wall or fence instead, equipped with sticks of wood of all sizes, shapelessly stuck to the walls and protruding from the walls and headed in various odd directions. These are crude wooden forms that in the morning will have a whole new look. Every skeletal shape and structure reminds me of how incredibly hard the Guatemalans must work every single day just to survive. Yet they smile through everything and greet every stranger who is receptive with a cheerful "hola" or "buenos dias" and you can truly feel their love and caring in the way you are greeted. It's like they don't just "say" the words, the mean what they say.

In the morning I love to sit at my favorite restaurant and watch the village come to life. The heavy metal doors roll up to reveal amazing splashes of brilliantly colored items that have been patiently crafted in dilapidated hovels that these smiling people call "home."

Gradually, what once were walls and fences covered with sticks of wood will become instead one shop after another that hadn't existed the night before except for the makeshift wooden skeletons. Once the morning is well underway the most magnificent array of colorful creations are displayed and covering every possible inch of the new little shops that are not shops at all but a brilliant array of handicrafts hanging on wooden skeletons. You can feel the cheerful spirits of these people, who are what's left of the ancient Mayan civilization. You can feel their cheerful spirits not only in their faces and demeanor but in the colors and beauty of their crafts.

I watch men, women and children pushing heavy carts filled with their only hope for survival – their handicrafts. They pass each other and the gringo tourists sharing smiles and good will. The hundreds of pounds of blankets, trinkets, handmade shoes, beaded jewelry, fabrics, tee shirts and an endless array of beauty are carefully and methodically arranged and the press to persuade passers-by to buy begins, bright and early. Not until well past dark will every piece of their beautiful unsold crafts be carefully stacked and again loaded into their carts so the village can go to sleep for a few hours and so these industrious Guatemalans can go to sleep for a little while as well.

The people in my village have every kind of problem we in the USA ever dreamed of having and more. They have to feed their families every day and, if they can, get them health care when they need it – if they can. They have their share of cheating husbands (and I suppose wives too) and there are children who have been abandoned by one or the other or both parents, just like in the USA. They have family members with terrible diseases, mental illness and addictions just like we do. They get old, sick and die. Just like we do. But I am not even going to tell you all the things that we have (good things) and they don't have because you already know or could easily guess.

The Guatemalans could certainly teach us all a thing or two about being happy in spite of things being less than perfect. They surely have taught me a thing or two about happiness. And they surely have made it more crystal clear to me than ever before how very grateful we should be for all the wonderful things we have in our country. Things that are so often taken for granted.

Everywhere in the world are people who, just by living their lives in their normal, everyday way, can teach us more about living, loving and appreciating than we are ever likely to learn staying home. Definitely, I do believe that travel should be a prerequisite to starting life. But I guess it's never too late, maybe? How about NOW?

PANAJACHEL, LAKE ATITLAN, GUATEMALA, MARCH 24, 2009
Yesterday I touched reality. Life may never be the same for me.

My little friend Elena is a few inches taller than I am. Well, that is when she is standing and I am sitting.

Elena is 14 years old and she has been trying to "close" me to buy something from her (anything) for over a month. She is soft-spoken and persistent but not pushy. Now that is not an easy way to be here when every quetzal (the Guatemalan dollar) is so important and so urgent to every single person.

The day before yesterday Elena came by where I was having dinner and finally closed me on a table runner. That day was Good Friday and all the locals were dressed to the nines (what does that mean, anyway?). Elena was wearing a skirt of the most magnificent fabric that she said her mother had woven by hand at their home. I had been looking at so many pieces of fabrics for weeks and I fell in love with Elena's skirt.

The skirts the ladies wear here (called a "corte") are very large tubes that they step into and wrap around themselves like a sarong. The looms they use are only about 20 to 24 inches wide. So to put together a tube of the proper size it's necessary to sew together two narrow pieces of hand woven fabric. All in all Elena´s skirt amounted to a usable piece of fabric about 40 inches wide and maybe 3 yards long.

Elena invited me to come to where she lives in Santa Catarina (another lakeside village) and meet her mother, who does all the weaving and everything else creative, I guess. Elena said her mother had other pieces of new fabric for me to look at and she kept urging me to visit her home by telling me how very beautiful it is where she lives. I couldn't think of any good reason not to go other than routine fear of the unknown – which by now I've gotten used to bumping up against and overcoming. So I told her to meet me the next morning at my regular breakfast place and I would go with her to her home.

She showed up right on time with a different skirt on. From what I have learned so far about Guatemalans, I was quite certain that Elena's skirt, that I had fallen in love with, was at her home awaiting a buyer.

A few minutes after Elena showed up at my restaurant, her brother arrived with a completely different product line. I guess they specialize. He was selling beautiful necklaces and pens with designs molded around them. The pens, I learned, were also the creations of the multi-talented mother. It seems if there is anything a person can use for anything at all, the Guatemalans will figure out a way to doll it up and bring it to your breakfast table to exchange for quetzals for their own or their kid's dinner. I bought pancakes and milk for Elena and Jose Daniel. I am certain Elena thanked me at least 10 times while she inhaled the pancakes.

After we had all finished eating there was much discussion about how we should get to Santa Catarina. Elena, being the practical one of the trio, was pushing for the back of a pickup truck, which is Panajachel's answer to the Rapid Transit District traditional "bus" in my cooontree. This method of transport is dirt cheap and would have cost less than a dollar for all three of us to reach our destination. While Santa Catarina is another lakeside village, for some reason people tend to travel there by road rather than ferry.

Jose Daniel was pushing for a tuk tuk. A tuk tuk is an adorable, mostly open air, three-wheeled vehicle that everybody scoots around town in. to me, tuk tuks seem more like large toys than anything serious. But they are extremely functional and an all around brilliant invention. They are the commonly accepted "taxi" mode of travel in all the villages around the lake, where there are roads, that is. I'm guessing that because Jose Daniel is only

10 years old, he thinks riding in a tuk tuk is way fun. Well, to be perfectly honest, so does this old great grandmother. That's probably because riding in a tuk tuk IS fun!

I tend to begin every adventure as a coward. As of yesterday I had not had the pleasure of standing up while racing down the street in the back of a pickup truck - yet. So I decided to cough up the just under $4 US fare for the three of us to have a fun ride in a tuk tuk.

We arrived after only about a ten minute journey in our tiny little tuk tuk, having traveled on a winding road in competition with chicken buses, cars, shuttles and trucks. But we made it quickly and safely and ended the easy part of the adventure at the foot of the steps of the Santa Catarina church. I got a little nervous when I noticed the entire village was on a rather steep hillside.

After I huffed and puffed to climb up stone steps just to get to the church, Elena disappeared around the side of the church. Following after her like a puppy, I eventually discovered she was ascending more steps. Us oldies really do tend to appreciate handrails in situations like this. Especially stone steps with irregular surfaces that have been worn down by hundreds of years of worshipers. The concept of handrails seems to be one that is unknown in Santa Catarina and something seldom considered in most places I've been around the lake. I continued to follow Elena up a very steep stairway that went straight up without the benefit of anything to hold onto.

I thought to myself, "If all these many stairs exist and I just got this far, only God knows how many more are in store for me!" It was at this moment that I began to truly fear for my sanity. This whole adventure is happening just because I fell in love with the fabric on little Elena's "corte."

As you may have guessed, we continued to traverse the hill, finding more and more steep handrail-less flights of steps, until finally I was sure I would be and maybe should be, committed to a mental hospital as soon as I step off the plane at LAX. That is if, in fact, I should live that long. Surviving this latest madness looked like a happy conclusion to this adventure that became more and more unlikely, the higher I ascended.

Every now and then Elena would sit on a wall in the shade and pat it, telling me to sit down and rest. I was afraid that if I sat I might have time to think. And if I thought, I might see more clearly the insanity in my decision to embark on this ludicrous adventure, just because I fell in love with Elena's "corte."

I would pause on a landing now and then and stare in awe at the magnificent view of the lake. When Elena would notice I was awe-struck with the view, she would once again tell me how beautiful it is where she lives. And, in fact, the sight of the lake when one is perched on her hillside is truly incomparable.

Jose Daniel ran on ahead of us as I kept asking in English, "Are we there yet?" I didn't know how to say that in Spanish but I was only talking to myself anyway, so it didn't really matter.

I finally saw Jose Daniel poke his head out from behind a jagged piece of corrugated metal. They both announced at once that we had arrived at their home. The beautiful home Elena had so proudly urged me to visit.

I felt like Elena wanted me to visit her home and meet her mother more than that she wanted me to buy something. In fact, it seemed the *most* important thing for her was that I had come all that way to her home to meet her mother.

When I stepped behind the makeshift corrugated metal gate I discovered that there was no house for Elena to live in at all. To the right was more corrugated metal about waist high that is fashioned into a sort of fence, with sticks of obviously local vegetation somehow involved in the design. This fence clearly appeared to serve no more useful purpose than say, "This is the end of our space."

Beyond the "sort of fence" was the most spectacular view of the lake. Lake Atitlan is truly a magnificent sight from any angle and on any day – foggy, sunny, windy or rainy. But on this particular day there was a crystal clear blue sky. The lake was at it's most spectacular. It's affect on me was like when I get a glimpse of a hummingbird hovering at a flower. The sight of the lake took my breath away. Well, what was left of my breath following the long ascent up the hill.

There were more children running around the sort of yard than Elena had reported as siblings. The day before this hike she had told me she was one of five and two were teenagers. They were not there at all. I suspected they were probably were already out working the restaurants in Panajachel. They were probably two of the many beautiful young women who had also been trying to "close" me for over a month. The other children were, as best I could figure out, cousins.

After almost tripping on the irregular terrain in the tiny yard and dodging the scattered stones, puddles and other obstacles, I finally made it to Elena's home and was welcomed like a valued friend who hadn't been by for a visit in a long time.

A large, tattered black plastic tarp was moved aside and I found myself in the main living space of the Cumez family. There is no floor. Only a continuation of the irregular dirt that was outside in the yard. But inside there was an absence of stones and other clutter. Clearly they had cleaned house for their honored guest.

I was in somewhat of a state of shock so my memory fails me a bit. But to my recollection there were maybe three cinder block walls that were about shoulder high and above them more corrugated metal. I don't have a clue what the roof was made of or how it was attached. I was only conscious of not being in the sun any longer and that was my only clue that there even was a roof.

Elena's mother showed me to a wooden seat along one wall upon which she had carefully placed a soft, white, obviously hand-made blanket. It was obvious that this seat had been arranged for their guest and I did, indeed, feel quite honored by the gesture.

Once again I find myself in an adventure where no English is spoken. And, once again, I am stunned to find myself somehow in communication with these lovely and hospitable people. Lovely people who don't enjoy even the luxury of a *level* surface of dirt under their bare feet to call home.

The mother, Maria of course is her name, shows me a few new "cortes" that she has woven herself, one thread at a time. She also shows me the just washed and still damp skirt that they have taken right off little Elena's person to prepare for their hopelessly insane prospect.

All this preparation, of course, in the hopes that I would turn out to be trustworthy enough to actually meet Elena between 9 and 10 a.m. and then that I would climb the endless steps to visit their humble home. Actually the word "humble" is almost too grand a word for where the Cumez family lives. And to believe that this space is "home" to these beautiful people very nearly tore my heart into a million pieces.

Knowing in our minds and with our intellect that people live such challenged lives is one thing. But to sit as a special guest on a snow white blanket, surrounded by dirt floor, corrugated metal, cinders blocks and a large tattered black tarp for a door – well, that is something you can see with your eyes or think in your brain. But you can only feel it in the torn parts around the edges of your broken heart.

Those of you who know me know that I buy my clothes at the thrift stores and then, preferably, on senior citizens days when I can get a substantial additional discount. You know that I am NOT the fashion diva of any neighborhood and that clothing would be the last item with any standing whatsoever on *my* budget.

Yet, I have been pricing these amazing fabrics that the indigenous Guatemalan ladies wear here and I am well aware of the endless hours that are involved in their creation. So imagine how shocked I am to find myself in a hovel, on a hillside, about to negotiate for a piece of cloth. Your friend Linda Lou, a person who is entirely content and happy in a $3 second-hand T-shirt and maybe even some third-hand, $5 blue jeans. And she has ascended to this height over a piece of fabric! I have just risked life and limb to involve myself in this madness – on purpose and of my own free will. Fancy that!

Maria begins the negotiation for my favorite, still damp corte at $1500 quetzals or around $200. She's not trying to cheat me or take advantage of me. She simply knows how much time it took for her to create Elena's skirt and she knows the going price for such items. And I fully respect every minute of her time. It's a complete mystery to me how it's possible to weave such incredible designs with just threads going in opposite directions.

I must respect Maria's time even more when the room is filled with children of all ages, who, I don't forget for one second, need to be tended to all day long. A space full of children who get hungry at regular intervals. Since there are more children than I know to be part of Maria's offspring, the best I can figure is that she is also caring for probably her own or her husband's sibling's children as well as her own sons and daughters. Having, as a young mother myself, attempted creative endeavors simultaneous to caring for children, and at that only two, I am fully aware of the challenges of this type of multitasking.

It's insane for me to think of spending $200 on a piece of cloth and even if I were THAT crazy, I didn't have that much money with me.

In the midst of our negotiation I noticed a man holding a baby in a dark windowless room just off the tiny main space. When he saw that I had noticed him he picked up the baby, (Elena had told me she has a 3 month old sister) and made his way rather slowly into the great room (8 by 8 feet of dirt floor, cinderblock walls and corrugated metal), where I sat as an honored guest on the snow white, hand-made blanket.

Mother Maria went off somewhere. To look for more product, I guess, and I asked the man if he worked in Santa Catarina. He said in Spanish that he had (past tense) and volunteered the name of his occupation. Unfortunately, I didn't understand the word he used to describe what his job had been, but he added that he is not currently working because he injured his spine and was not now able.

By this point, the room was filled with mother, father, little Elena and I don't even remember how many little kids. They were all looking at a crazy woman sitting on a snow white blanket who had climbed to the top of the hill (without benefit of handrails) for some un-Godly and insane reason that she herself could not comprehend.

I tried as best I could to explain to Maria how very understanding I was of the incredible amount of work that goes into weaving such a beautiful fabric by hand. I further tried in my ridiculous Spanish to explain that I am a retired old woman who is not rich and I couldn't possibly spend that much money on a piece of cloth. No matter how much I loved and appreciated it, how beautiful it was or how much work it took to create it.

The more I talked and resisted, the more the reality of life for this little family sunk into my fractured heart via my befuddled brain.

Maria finally agreed to sell the cloth to me for $1200 quetzals. I bravely continued to carry on about how I just couldn't do it. Then I started looking hard at each one of those kids and I started thinking what it would mean to their lives for me to buy that damp piece of cloth.

They were all so cheerful. They were smiling and laughing and completely unaware that life could be one bit different than it is for them, every day of their lives. I started thinking about little Elena taking the skirt right off her body so that her mother could wash it and sell it to me. I thought about her going to school and descending and ascending those steps every day. And after school getting in the back of a pickup truck, all by herself or with her little brother Jose Daniel, to travel to another village and be brushed off and rejected hour after hour, day after day, year after year by pudgy tourists like myself, feeding their faces.

In those moments of indecision, my life and my heart expanded far beyond the distance from California to Guatemala. I knew then why I had come to Guatemala. I knew why I had stayed, even after my Joey died. I knew why

I had climbed to the top of that hill on steep steps with no rail. I knew why there was more money in my backpack than I probably should have brought. And I didn't fail to think about the shortage in my own meager budget that I would create if I spent what I had with me frivolously on a damp piece of cloth.

I didn't come to the top of this hill to spend the quetzals. I came to touch reality. I came to see how people can make a difference in the lives of their fellow humans. No. I didn't come to see it, because I could see it in a book or a movie and I had done that many, many times. I came to FEEL, first hand, the real human conditions that most of us in our comfortable lives in the USA never will bump up against accept in movies, on TV and in books. We will encounter facsimiles of reality to explore in our minds. Not in our hearts. Only by sitting on that snow white blanket with my feet on the dirt floor could I truly touch reality. And on that good day, just following Good Friday, I did just that.

That morning the ATM on Calle Santander had spit out brand new, crisp 100 quetzales bills. I finally brought out a bunch of them and said, "OK. 1200." At the same time, some chunk of my brain was screaming, "You are crazy. Completely nuts. You're a fool. You've been hypnotized." But my brain had no say in the matter as it was clearly my heart giving the instructions to count out and hand over the money.

As I counted and Maria saw that I only had 1200 quetzals and was about to give her every quetzal I had, she suddenly said, "No. 1000 because you are my friend." So I handed her 10 crisp 100Q bills and returned 2 more to my purse. Enough to eat for a few days if I'm careful.

Suddenly, everyone was thrilled, happy and the language barrier continued to be only a minor challenge. Communication was working perfectly!

Maria wanted to give me food and drink. I was pretty stuffed as I had just finished breakfast when Elena found me at Pana Rock, Lake Atitlan's version of the Hard Rock Café. So I declined the hospitable offer both because I didn't think I could eat a bite and also because, while I was sure my hosts were accustomed to the microbes of their own neighborhood cuisine, I was pretty sure my sissy intestines were not.

After the deal had been struck and they were all joyous and convinced I was not going to eat or drink, I told them I must have pictures of them all because I always take picture of the people I buy anything from. Getting them all scrunched in together, while carefully displaying my new piece of cloth was not an easy task. Finally, I got a few pictures but most of them were blurry. I feared everyone would scatter if I stopped to re-adjust the camera settings so I quit shooting at about 5 pictures.

I asked if they had an address so I could send them copies of the pictures later. The papa got a huge piece of paper and began to write. But before he had formed one letter he instead asked me if I would do it. I don't think Nicholas knows how to write. More chunks fell off the edges of what was left of my heart.

I have one picture of my father's family when Daddy was a teenager. He was the oldest boy of 12 children. Just one picture. That's it. I had heard many stories of how poor my father's family had been. How they had taken the labels off cans of food to stick on the walls so they might stop cold air from blowing through cracks in the walls of shacks they would live in as they wandered from farm to farm, picking whatever vegetables or fruits needed picking. My father's family was poor. Very poor. Maybe even poorer than the Cumez family who at least have a permanent place to live.

A place that hopefully the next rains will not wash away into the lake as had happened in another Atitlan village not far from Santa Catarina.

I always understood in my brain what my father life was about. But until I looked at the blurry pictures in the window of the camera and saw that little family with their feet on the dirt floor of their home, I don't think I ever really "got it". I don't think I ever really felt what my own father's life as a child had really been. I "got it" at that moment when I saw the Cumez family in the camera. I had time for a quick flash of what it must have taken for my father to climb out of his plight with no education - barely able to read. After being a character from straight out of *The Grapes of Wrath*, he managed, with nothing but his own strength, will and intentions to build a life for himself and his own family. I touched even my own reality on that steep hillside.

I thought to myself, "When I send these pictures to my new friends, they may be the only pictures they will ever have of their whole family, smiling and so happy together."

With the help of a cousin, we went outside and took a few more pictures with the beautiful lake in the background. I was standing to Maria's left. Elena was to her right. Elena reached behind her mother and took my right arm. She brought it around and put it over her mother's shoulder and then held onto my hand while her cousin pushed the button on the camera. That particular friendly arrangement for that picture was very important to Elena, for reasons only she will ever understand.

When I said goodbye to the Nicolas and Maria Cumez family of Calle Vista Hermosa (beautiful view street) I didn't feel $132 poorer. I felt a million times richer than rich.

101

The departure plan to return to Panajachel was that Jose Daniel would come down the hill with Elena and me but he would not be going back to work in Panajachel. He was to run back home – up the hundreds of steps without rails. But Elena would get back to Panajachel where she would work the restaurants for the rest of the day and try to earn a few more cents selling her mother's handiwork to keep her little family alive.

Going down the steps was far more frightening than going up since going up I didn't see where I could end up if I were to fall. On the way down I could see clearly how I might tumble to my doom. Where while climbing and watching every step, I could only image what the fall might be. But I had the help of my two little friends to steady me and we went very slowly - together.

The steps were not wide enough to have a helper on each side of me so I said only one helper would be enough. I didn't stop to think that Elena had been the central character in this adventure throughout. But somehow I made the descent with Jose Daniel holding my hand for most of the trip while Elena followed behind us mumbling to him in some ancient Mayan language. She was obviously annoyed at him for something. I had no clue what.

When we reached the bottom of all those steps, Elena was very sad and she wouldn't say why. I think she felt jealous because Jose Daniel had been the one who mostly helped me get down the stairs.

For the sake of economy which, again Elena was pushing for, we planned to take a pickup back to Panajachel. However, we got lucky and a wonderfully comfortable van took us back to Pana instead for the same price as a pickup truck would have charged. Just a few cents if I recall.

When we got back to the main drag in Panajachel, Elena was still sad about something but she wouldn't say what. When I asked if it was about not having her corte anymore she just laughed as if the corte meant nothing to her. I was a bit baffled so I got a banana split, which we shared like a couple of girlfriends. I assure her that she was my friend and that she was a wonderful girl for taking me to her home and for giving up her beautiful skirt. I told her that what she did was very, very good for her family and she should be very happy. That reassurance and the banana split seemed to help a bit. But Elena couldn't stop asking me if I would come to visit her home again. She wanted to "close" me about when I would be there again.

The sight of the endless steps was still so clear in my mind so that all I could say was maybe, maybe, maybe.

Now the question is, what will I do with that ridiculously expensive piece of cloth? I'll bet you can tell that this story is not about the money or the cloth, can't you?

PANAJACHEL, LAKE ATITLAN, GUATEMALA, MARCH 31, 2008

This is Linda Lou signing off on the **Guatemala** circuit for this particular adventure. On Wednesday, April 2, 2008 at 8:20 p.m., my flight leaves **Guatemala City** for LAX. So I will be home, not that I actually have a home, on April 3rd.

One last message to catch up on the continuing saga of life in Guatemala. First I must say I am surely going to miss being here. Every day I try very hard to understand why that would be. It's true the view of the lake is quite spectacular. But I don't spend my days gazing upon the beauty of the lake. I look at it "sometimes" but there's so much more to it than that.

So what's the attraction around here? We have pretty stunning noise pollution here in Pana and since there doesn't seem to be an air pollution control district, we could just say that air quality leaves LOTS to be desired. It's not so bad if you try not to breathe too deeply in the street.

Then there's the traffic sometimes. To take a walk down Santander (the main drag), one must be willing to place one's life in God's hands. There simply is no other way. There are no sidewalks and the surface of the streets is fascinating. No need to place cones around the many, many open holes as every step is pretty much at your own risk anyway.

Structures are mostly rather tacky. Unless, that is, you go to some gringo's house and then you might believe you are in Beverly Hills with fabulous stone walls, magnificent gardens, giant bathtubs and stunning views of the lake.

So what would it be that I am going to miss you might ask? As I said, that's a question I ask myself daily. So here is my take on it in a nutshell?

People.

Imagine a small town where, when you walk down the street, your neighbors smile at you – pretty much without exception – and say "Good morning. How are you?" And they even truly care how you are. Even the neighbors you don't know. It's archaic behavior I tell you! It's simply not done in my country anymore.

Imagine a place where almost everyone you see is smiling. I so wonder what it is that the locals are smiling about. Like, do they know something they are not telling me? Maybe they tell more jokes around here than anywhere else in the world. Could that be it? I truly don't know. Or maybe they are just in the habit of being happy, even though they have the most difficult lives I can imagine. What kind of lesson is there in that idea? Be happy no matter what!!!

Here's an example. You recall my little friend Elena? That Saturday that I climbed all those jillion steps to visit her family a week or so ago. That was the day I lost my mind from altitude sickness, I suppose. And then, after that insane ascent I impetuously spent $132 for a piece of cloth. Recall Elena's family is dirt poor. So you can imagine how shocked and touched I was when a few days after that visit Elena showed up at Pana Rock, my favorite breakfast place, all smiles and with gifts for ME! She was so overjoyed because her mother had sent her to find me and give me two beautiful necklaces and a pen that her mother had decorated beautifully with designs all around it, including a frog and a fish.

For such dirt poor and uneducated people to have the grace of such gratitude made me realize what a special place I had come to. No wonder it is so difficult for me to leave here.

Since Elena is fourteen, I had presumed that she might be able to send me a letter now and then and she even told me that she would. But I had not been able to determine if Elena actually does know how to read and write. If she could read and write I had thought I would leave her my dictionary to help her learn English. So I had been trying to establish her level of literacy before my departure. One morning I put my notebook and a pen in front of her as she was enjoying the pancakes I had ordered for her. I have learned that breakfast is a rare treat for many of the children selling in the streets here. I asked Elena to write one sentence for me. She formed one letter, "O," and that was it. She just stopped. I thought maybe she just didn't know what to write and since we do have a pretty substantial language barrier between us, I gave up trying to satisfy my curiosity for that particular moment.

A few days after that experience I met with Estella, my Spanish teacher. We had grown quite fond of each other and she had come all the way across the lake by ferry to give me a Spanish lesson. We were about to have lunch near the lake when we happened upon Elena. So the three of us went to lunch. I asked my Spanish teach to help me find out if Elena could or could not read and write. Estella also speaks the local language of Ketchekal so I thought that might help too. Even with no language barrier whatsoever, it still took Estella some time to get to the truth. I think Elena was perhaps embarrassed to come right out and tell it like it is.

In the end, it was confirmed that fourteen year-old Elena has only gone to school for three years in her entire life and that, in fact, she cannot read and write. I was heartbroken and speechless when I realized that truth. Yet, this shy, sweet, grateful, well mannered young girl is sent out into the streets of Panajachel every day to sell her mother's handicrafts. With Estella my translator to help me, I also learned that if Elena doesn't sell anything while she is out working the streets, the family will often not have food for that day. With that news I bought scarves I didn't want or need immediately. I discovered that there are, actually five "children" still at home in Elena's family but in total her mother had seven children. Two sisters are gone from their home.

Before we lunched at the lake, I had seen Elena a few times and noticed that she had a cold. She was coughing frequently, but never failed to turn her head and cover her mouth. This young girl's beautiful manners, including her sweet table manners, would put so many young people I've seen in the USA to shame.

Yesterday I was sitting with Elena and she told me something like this: "Mi madre necessita estupida hacer tortillas." To me that meant, "My mother needs a stupid woman to make tortillas." That made no sense at all so I asked her over and over in every way I could think of what she was saying. I finally gave up and looked around for someone to interpret for me. Once I found someone who could follow the story, it turned out that what she was actually saying was that her mother needs a stove to make tortillas. The mysterious word that was causing the communication problem was not estupida (stupid woman) but instead was "estufa" (stove). The cost of a stove just happens to be 1000 quetzales or $132 - the exact amount I paid her mother for Elena's skirt. Elena told me it would take at least a year for them to get that much money for a stove. That's when I realized how much the money I gave her mother, in my moment of altitude sickness, must have really meant to them. So I asked Elena what her mother had done with the money for her skirt and she informed me that it paid for her younger brothers to go to school for two more months and for food and clothes for the family. If things weren't bad enough they must even pay here for their children to go to school.

Definitely, it's the people here in Panajachel that make it so hard for me to leave.

There are so many things that people need in Guatemala and so many ways that they have suffered from civil turmoil, killings and natural disasters – to name a few. This country has been an opportunity for exploitation by bad guys from all over the world. But it is also a wonderful opportunity for people from all over the world who know they are far better off in their own lives than the indigenous Guatemalans. It's a wonderful place for those folks with such good intentions to find outlets for their generosity. What a magnificent reason to take up residence in a country such as Guatemala. To help the indigenous people of so many lands to have better lives by teaching them things that will help them earn more money and have better lives. Like teaching English. Even a little English could be so meaningful in helping the kids selling their mother's masterpieces to make more money to take home to feed the family or pay for more schooling for them.

On leaving I am also reflecting on not only the indigenous people who are very, very special but also the foreigners who come to stay here that are amazing as well.

Imagine a place where when you run into a friend in the street – that is, a friend who is from some country other than Guatemala – you can be pretty sure that that person is on his or her way to engage in some act of benevolence. Almost without exception, the expats I meet here and have become friends with are deeply involved in helping the Guatemalans have better lives in some way or another. When there is so much need everywhere, you might believe that being involved in helping would be a snap. But it is not. Challenges abound.

For example you cannot simply hand over money to the kids and say, "Take this home for food." It is not unlikely that the food money you give them will get into the hands of people (the unemployed fathers for example) who may use it to get drunk or use drugs. Yet being here you can fully understand why a man might want to get drunk and escape the endless frustrations he must face every day.

You cannot simply say, "Well, I will set up a school and help to educate these good and deserving children." Things don't cost that much here so there is a temptation to do that sort of thing because it is financially "do-able." Many people work diligently to make such endeavors successful. However, people tell me all the time that the kids might show up or not.

And not necessarily because they don't want to be educated but perhaps, as in Elena's case, because they are needed to instead go out and earn money in the streets peddling the handicrafts that their mothers are making back in their hovels. Also they may not show up because they don't understand the concept of their lives being any better if they become educated. And their parents – also not educated – may not understand that concept either. How could they possibly know what education might mean to them since it is difficult to watch American television when you don't have electricity and are busy in the streets selling to tourists?

Not only are the above problems with the indigenous people showstoppers, there are also the endless power struggles between the volunteers who are running organizations designed to help people. Volunteers who are truly putting their hearts and souls into helping. Organizations, just because they are worthy causes, are never devoid of problems and ego trips. It's difficult, I am told, to position one's self in a worthy cause when someone must be in charge, but everyone is a volunteer and no one is getting paid. It's more complicated than we might think.

Still, to be among such a group of expats who are struggling – no matter what the challenges – to better the lives of others less fortunate than themselves, is a pretty wonderful place to be.

Yes, it surely is the people here I will miss.

And then there's the tuk tuks. I must admit I do love the tuk tuks.

> *To me every hour of the day and night is*
> *an unspeakably perfect miracle.*
>
> -   **Walt Whitman**

THREE
Why on Earth?

Tourists don't know where they've been, travelers don't know where they're going.

- **Paul Theroux**

-

Having gotten through an authentic run down of just one extended, travel adventure (as opposed to being a tourist at a five star) you may now be more or less inclined to want to fill up a backpack and take off to parts unknown, particularly on a shoestring. If your interest is peaked at all and you still suffer from a little twinge of wanderlust, now begins the parts where I am going to grind on you to get going.

If after the scorpions, frantic ferries and insane fabric shopping on a hillside of heady heights have had the opposite effect on you, this is a good stopping off point. You might just be saying, "Hell no. I won't go!" Well, that's totally understandable too. You might just hand the book over to your restless friends who still want to see the world no matter what. This may be a good point to give up the exercise of continuing this read because from here on I'll be out to convince you that you simply DO NOT want to stay home one minute longer than absolutely necessary.

First, I must admit I spent much of my professional life (25 + years of it anyway) in a sales capacity of one type or another. So you must forgive me if this book from time to time seems to be a sales pitch for *something*.

Well, truth is, this IS a sales pitch. And here come the features, advantages and benefits of worldwide travel and adventure. NOW.

Many people just want to go. They don't really stop to think about what exactly they expect to get from the experience. They just have the itch and long to scratch it with passports, tickets, guide books and whatever it takes. If so, don't worry about why. Just GO!

I've talked with countless people from all over the world who have taken off for faraway lands and are living their lives outside the box. Here are some things they have told me they have gotten from travel. And, I'm betting this list barely scratches the surface of what is the least you can expect from taking the plunge. Scary plunge or not.

SELF CONFIDENCE AND INCREASED SELF ESTEEM. If the thought of taking off into the unknown is a bit intimidating but ultimately you do it anyway, nothing is more likely to make you feel very confident and really good about yourself than travel. Surviving your first adventure will most definitely give you a positive view of your own abilities to survive, thrive and create your own fun. Especially good for confidence building are shoestring and extended travel because your opportunities to be resourceful will be many, varied and often highly challenging.

I don't know for sure but I'm thinking the people who have money enough to send their kids off for extended travel before they start going away to college, do it for some very practical reason and not just entertainment for the kids. I'm thinking the benefits hoped for when sending the kids off include such things as learning to be strong, self-reliant, resourceful and self-confident.

FUN. As I explained previously, my mother always chastised me as a kid, saying, "All you want to do is have fun." It always sounded as if it was some kind of sin to want to have fun. Well, I don't know where she got

112

such wild ideas. But thank God I grew up in the era of *"Father Knows Best."* The good news is my father was an advocate of having fun. I just picked the training that felt the best and in this case, "Father DEFINITELY Knew Best" as far as I was concerned. I'm going with his lessons and I am inviting you to do the same.

Set out to have fun for the rest of your life. And truly, if we can get all our noses to the grindstones theories put aside, and since it surely is time to do that once we retire, who doesn't want to have fun? It so beats the alternatives. So why not?

Truth is, travel can be tons of fun (and usually is for me). Frankly I wouldn't mind just doing it all the time.

LOVE. There are quite a few things to think about in the pursuit of love. First, and maybe most important, is the concept that before anyone will love you, you must first learn to love yourself. I'm going to allude to the possibility that with enough self-confidence and permission to have fun and be fun, you will far more easily learn to love yourself. Being in a state of self-love is an outstanding beginning for one's Golden Years. In the Golden Years the most important person you must take care of is yourself. And loving the person for whom you are caretaker seems like a really great idea to me!

I'm not talking about egomania with this self-love stuff. I'm only suggesting you see the reality of yourself with all your great qualities and accomplishments. And I'm suggesting you appreciate them as much as you would appreciate the same qualities in someone else.

113

Then, walk this wonderful planet in a state of confidence and fun. If you wander through life loving yourself with every step, you will be amazed how people of all ages will want to hang out in your company.

If you are looking for romantic love, that's certainly a great possibility along the way as well. When you are "out there," having fun, creating romantic love will be far more likely for you to encounter than when confined in your living room with only your TV to love you.

If romantic love is of no interest, who on earth is going to complain about an abundance of platonic love. In this case I refer to the love expressed in many other countries just because the indigenous people of certain cultures happen to come from that *way of being*. This will not be true no matter where you go. So you will have to do some research on your destinations to find out if you might be encountering whole cultures of loving people. That is, if hanging out with large groups of loving people is what floats your boat.

In countries or areas where indigenous people tend to be very loving (like Bali and Guatemala for example), you will see it manifested in very mundane ways. For example, try something as simple as frequenting the same little café every day for a few days. You might be surprised to discover the way the people who bring you coffee and breakfast or an afternoon cocktail will love to see you show up repeatedly. Just showing up regularly will tell them that you want to be their friend and in no time you will be treated accordingly. It is so simple, really. Just show up every morning for a few days. It will make your servers smile just to be able to say, "Your usual?" Sounds like a small thing, but sure makes for a lot of great feelings on both sides of the encounter.

This is one of the many reasons I love to stay in a place for as long as possible or as long as my visa will allow, rather than checking out all the ruins and museums in two days, moving on to examine the next pile of ancient or interesting "stuff" and missing the beauty of the local altogether. My feelings about travel are not to see how many imprints I can plant on my aging brain of "things" I've seen. I can fill my brain with sights by watching TV and not have to scratch at mosquito bites. My interest is in getting a real sense of what it *feels* like to live in a place – to BE there. I want to know what it *feels* like to be a resident and know the locals. And maybe even try to become one of them. In so many places it truly is as simple as just showing up.

If you figure out a way to stay in one place for weeks with the persona of a confident and fun-loving character, or better yet, hang out for months at a time, you will be amazed at how the locals (including foreigners who have become locals) will just hate to see you go. You'll have so many new friends you won't know which way to turn.

COMPANIONSHIP. Along similar lines, if you are looking for companionship, this brings to mind again my theory that you are better off traveling solo than with a travel companion. Sounds a bit contradictory, doesn't it? But in truth it is a rare day that a solo traveler doesn't encounter other travelers with an interest in exchanging stories. And, if you are out there with a spirit of fun and adventure you are pretty much guaranteed to run into fellow travelers who are likely to be interested in wandering off on some mini adventures with you. It's just part of the travel culture. Remember, that's "travel" not "vacation" culture. More on this later.

Many people, who typically would not approach a stranger in a shopping mall in the USA and start a conversation, find it so very simple to get acquainted with fellow travelers. In fact, if you stay in other than huge five star hotels, you will find that it's almost impossible NOT to get to know the other travelers you encounter. They will be sincerely interested in where you have been or where you are going next. They will want to know what you have seen that they might learn something about so they can go there too. If you ask other travelers you encounter in your hostel, hotel or around town these same questions, they will immediately jump at the chance to share their adventures with you and offer any guidance or first-hand experience that they feel might make your future travels easier for you. It's a rare traveler who is not instantly willing to talk travel with a fellow traveler. It's not impossible to find such a person. But it IS rare.

In fact, it is so easy to talk to strangers when shoestring traveling that on a recent trip to Costa Rica, I actually had to specifically track down a deserted bungalow where NO people would be so that I could spend over a week in isolation putting the finishing touches on this book. Without exception, at every single place I stayed in Costa Rica (none of which cost more than $25 a night) there were so many wonderful new people to quickly and easily make friends with that it was absolutely impossible for me to make any progress at all in working on this book. The temptation to just hang out with new and wonderful people from all over the world was just too hard for me to resist since I'm such a sucker for a good time.

When you are traveling with a companion, the easiest thing in the world to do it chat all the time with the same companion you left home with. This will simply deprive you of the opportunity to engage with new and fascinating folks. Maybe it's just human nature to take the easy route and take along your own entertainment. Doesn't mean meeting fellow travelers along the way will not happen if you travel in tandem. It just will take a little more effort on your part to reach out of your comfort zone with your regular travel companion and find reasons to develop new relationship with people you meet along the way.

EDUCATION. I suspect that by the time we reach the age of retirement we all realize that the absolute dumbest thing we can do is decide we know all there is to know or anyway all there is that we, personally, need to know. Dumb, dumb, dumb. The older and wiser we get the clearer it should become to us that we know so little. We can never afford to stop learning and there is a limit to what we are going to learn by just spending our Golden Years like a hamster in a cage, shut in and running in circles but never moving forward. Now that we have the time to do what we want and a lifetime of mental foundation to build on, our minds should be more sponge-like than ever before. Now we don't have to fill our brain cells with corporate information, propaganda, job descriptions, financial considerations, schemes to advance in our careers, endless schedules, office politics, worries about the kids, etc. Now is our time to fill our grey matter with what *we choose* to care about. What we choose to learn. Not what we *have* to care about and learn to do what we *have* to do.

Whatever it is that you find fascinating, there is more of it to be absorbed by getting out of your comfort zone and into the rest of the world.

Without question, travel can be the greatest education in the world. And it's all there for the taking.

CLOSER TO GOD. This is not, by any means, a book on spiritual guidance. I got all the spiritual guidance I have ever been able to use from my father when I was about six. That would be the same father who came from a childhood of abject poverty and only a sixth grade education yet strongly believed in having fun. Daddy told me everything in one sentence

117

and, after many, many years of my own spiritual search, I have only been able to conclude that, once again, father knew best. He told me, simply, that, "God is everywhere and in everything we see." I'm going with that particular theory because it suits me. And who knows - maybe it's even true. This book is just not the place to find out. But the theory certainly makes a good case for seeing the world, if God truly is everywhere!

And I realize that such a simple theory wouldn't suit everybody. So if, in addition to your sparse wardrobe and light backpack, you carry along a very open mind, then whatever spiritual ideas or pursuits you already have will most certainly be challenged and/or validated on the road - just in the process of living "outside the box."

All the different cultures you encounter and the many fascinating travelers you meet along the way will offer new and at least interesting ways of looking at spirituality. Some new ideas you might decide to embrace, some may make you simply laugh and others may cause you to say, "Ah ha! Just as I suspected!" Whatever the case may be, there will be banquets of food of spiritual thought out there waiting for you to indulge to your hearts delight.

Another very simple aspect to travel that may bring one closer to God is the occasional feeling of terror while on the roads of foreign lands. I recall a special day of meeting my maker while riding on the back of a motor scooter on the island of Java in Indonesia.

I was traveling for a few days with a young Chinese fellow from Canada who was globe-trotting for a year but whose apparently successful at-home profession was that of "juggler." How many Chinese jugglers on sabbatical have you run into lately? Only on the road do such things seem to happen.

I had met Steve on the flight from Singapore to Jakarta and we decided to travel together for a few days as it happened we both were headed through the island of Java via train and bus to eventually end up on the magical island of Bali. Steve was in search of a sort of mystical massage therapist who could help him resolve some past life issues that he felt were causing him to have unwanted and inexplicable body pains. Steve had picked up a rumor in his travels that he might find such a healer in Java.

Steve and I were staying Yogjakarta on the island of Java for a few days. One day we were climbing through Borobudur, a huge ancient Buddhist pyramid sort of affair which also happens to be one of the official Wonders of the Ancient World. We wandered through hundreds of stone carvings shaped like hollow bells, each with a statue of Buddha inside. In time we came upon a pair of tour guides, one of whom told us that his wife's mother's, neighbor's aunt was reported to have these special mystical healing massage skills that Steve sought. The tour guides offered to take us on their motor scooters to the potential healer after we finished experiencing that particular exhausting world wonder, Borobudur. We could find this magic massage for Steve with their help and of course for a small fee. It's a kind of tricky tour guide technique one must learn to watch out for. After leading us up and down endless crude stone stairways and ramps in the world wonder (no hand rails, of course) for a few hours, off we went on our wild chase in pursuit of the mystical healer. And a wild chase it was.

At the time of this wild chase I was quite plump. Climbing on the motor scooter I realized I weighed much more than the driver. Maybe even more than the scooter and driver combined as the scooter wasn't much more than a motorized bicycle! I was clinging to the lightweight scooter driver for dear life throughout every second of the trip. Yet off we sped, fearlessly darting through heavy, wild Javanese traffic. I held my breath as my tiny

Indonesian scooter driver maneuvered us between buses and trucks that were racing in opposite directions. I was afraid to even flinch lest our top heavy condition might cause us to lose our balance, leaving us crumpled in a pile of bones and blood on that busy Indonesian street. All I could think about was the heart attack my mother would surely have if she could have seen where I was and what I was up to.

It's during peak experiences such as this that one has real opportunity to cozy up so much closer to God. I had experienced hair-raising traffic in many other countries before this, but it was not until that wild scooter ride in Java that I truly learned to turn my will and my life over to the hands of God.

This experience happened during the first week of a two month visit to Indonesia. While every experience on busy Indonesian roads is hair-raising, I had learned from Mr. Scooter's Wild Ride to simply put my life in God's hands and know that everything was going to turn out perfectly. And, that if I didn't survive that would be perfect too as it would no doubt be part of God's plan for me.

This new found trust made life so much more serene for me, although I do not by any means encourage such foolhardy behaviors. I see that wild ride strictly as a learning experience and now that I've learned and shared my learning with you, please accept my guidance and DON'T DO anything even remotely as dangerous.

RESPECT. If you turn out to be the one in your social circle who decides to load up your backpack (lightly) and take off, then here's a little warning you should receive and advance info you should know. Expect to hear a lot of noise from your stay-at-home peers, many of whom will go to almost any lengths to deter your designs on globe-trotting. But amazingly, along with their efforts to convince you it's a crazy idea, once you take the plunge and return victorious, you will then find yourself in a brand new place. You will become a kind of hero in your friend's eyes.

They may adamantly declare, "Oh, he's crazy to be doing that at this age," or, "I would never do anything like that. I just have no need to see anything but the good old USA. I have everything I need right here. I'm perfectly content."

Until recently I would have taken those kinds of comments as simply excuses to stay put. Maybe, I used to think, it's just a normal rationalization for avoiding fear. Rather one way and opinionated of me, don't you think? But my ongoing good fortune has more recently given me an opportunity to explore the truth and sanity in such attitudes. For well over a year I have had an opportunity to hang out peacefully in a beautiful California setting with endless gardens and projects to keep me busy and content. This has given me a wonderful awakening that has enabled me to see both sides of the question. To travel or not to travel? That is the question. And everyone's answer is most definitely not the same for a multitude of reasons.

I understand now that for many, no, probably most people of retirement age, all those stay at home concepts are absolutely perfect and right on. For most, that is. But not for all. If you want to go, don't stay home. If you really want to stay home – just do it!

Gaining the respect of your peers is not, in my opinion, any reason at all to travel or not travel. If you don't have the itch and a pretty strong urge to scratch it, nothing that has to do with other people's opinions could possibly serve as justification to hop on an airplane – or not.

If you do decide to travel, respect is just a little side perk that you will notice when you return and start sharing all your wonderful stories, photos and little trinkets with the folks back home.

ENLIGHTENMENT. – Don't you just love the experience of "ah ha!" Epiphanies are such quick and stunning moments in life that can shift a person's positions, beliefs, points of view, emotions, attitudes and so much more. Epiphanies can totally transform a person's entire life.

In my opinion, one of the greatest qualities us humans can have is being open to epiphanies. And there is no greater place to bump up against them than on the road, especially while hanging out in other cultures.

I once knew someone who would argue the concept of "right" and "wrong" for hours, insisting that both actually existed. For him it was a closed case. Black and white. And that is true for most people. This brilliant person, a distinguished professor of such lofty subjects as comparative anatomy and circadian rhythms, could not grasp my position that right and wrong are simply an aspect of the individuals "point of view." While I do realize and acknowledge that the matter of right and wrong is a very complex issue, I must also share about this individual's shift in his own point of view on returning from a one year sabbatical in the back countries of both Australia and New Guinea. After visiting with and somehow becoming quite closely involved in the social circles of some very primitive cultures, this brilliant individual return to the USA clear that right and wrong are, in fact, relative only to one's personal point of view. And where we should happen upon our point of view is quite a personal matter. For me that transformation of attitude represents epiphany at it's best. It's the kind of enlightenment that one is simply unlikely to experience without breaking out of his or her own cultural shell.

THRILLS. I've heard some very conflicted theories about what people are really looking for in life. For example, I heard a theory that people don't enjoy gambling because they might win, but rather, because they might lose. Seems it's the thrill of maybe losing that really does it for the gambler. And isn't it amazing that the movies we love the most, scare us to death because they are filled with things we would NEVER want to happen to us? Or that the evening news story we are inclined to follow with the most avid interest is the one that is filled with the most sensational details and usually is full of bad or dangerous happenings?

What is more fun than an amusement park where we love to get on rides that give us a very few minutes of feeling like they are our last few minutes?

It's true of an awful lot of people, especially when we reach the Golden Years, that we are inclined to arrange for more tranquility than we used to long for in our thirties. But we're not dead yet and many of us (maybe sometimes secretly) still love the excitement of thrilling stuff.

When my mother was over ninety she said she would just love to get on a really great roller coaster. She never insisted we arrange for such an event. And we never took her on such an outing because we didn't want to be responsible for her having a stroke or a heart attack over at Magic Mountain. But she thought about it and talked about it. We have often thought, since she passed away, that we should scatter her ashes from the highest point on the grandest roller coaster we could find. I realize that's probably terribly illegal and we would not actually do such a thing. But we have thought about it, nonetheless, because we figured if she knew, it would make her happy.

Should you make the big decision to become a Golden Years vagabond, the level of thrills you can expect is unlimited and truly very much in your own hands. The level of thrills you decide on will not be dependent on your budget as much as it will depend on your tastes and you ability to do some thorough research on potential destinations.

The very important **_Get Smart and Get Going_**, will provide a wealth of information about the importance of getting computer literate, NOW. Even if you never leave your block, it sure can't hurt to jump on the high tech band wagon and surf around on the World Wide Web. Lord knows we have more time to poke around on keyboards now that we're retired.

It's certainly true that one can travel endlessly without ever visiting a single website or sending a single email. You could do it the old fashioned way by reading books and talking on the phone to travel agencies, etc. That, however, would manifest a lot more thrills than even *I,* the promoter of all these wild ideas, would be willing to look forward to because I doubt you could put together as careful a plan by patch working your adventures together that way. The way I see it, control of your taste for thrills lives on the World Wide Web. Just decide what floats your boat and all the answers and directions are right there waiting for you to plan a perfectly grand, relatively safe and very thrilling itinerary. If you choose to.

EXERCISE. If there is one thing us seniors need desperately, its exercise. The wonderful thing about travel, especially if you want to really be a vagabond, is you don't have to go one bit out of your way to get more exercise than you ever dreamed possible. It's just part of the deal.

First, there's weight lifting galore. Because no matter how lightly you think you are going to pack that backpack, I promise, it won't happen. Well, not on your first trip anyway. Since everyone around you is busy carrying their own bags it's pretty certain you will get to do a fair amount of weight lifting – of your own bags. (As an added benefit to lifting bags, it's a wonderful teacher of what not to bring next time.) You might as well start practicing weight lifting now, just in case you really do this. If you don't go, so what? You'll still be feeling better and fitter than ever with every pound you lift.

Count on plenty of stair stepper action. Depending on how many thrills you build into your adventures I can promise you will encounter more stairs (maybe without rails) than escalators and elevators. Well, that is if you are planning to travel on a shoestring and have a taste for the more exotic stuff of life. If you've got more money than you know what to do with you just won't get much exercise unless you go to the health club at the five star. But all that must be in some other book. This book's about shoestring travel (see Chapter 17 - Spa Living for the joys of affordable spa life in case you don't have buckets of money.) Shoestring travel is guaranteed to provide plenty of exercise of all kinds.

Speaking of stairs, don't be too shy or embarrassed to take a collapsible walking stick. You can always be a little cocky with it – like look threatening. Sort of like, "Don't mess with me. I've got a stick and I know what to do with it!" Of course, if some really bad dude wanted to mess with you, let's face it, you'd be toast. But that is safety logic. And remember, it is less likely that such a thing will happen with the bad guys than that you'll get in a wreck on the freeway on the way to the podiatrist's office. The good thing about the walking stick is that if you should encounter an abundance of "rail-less" stairs or unfriendly surfaces, you will not be one bit sorry to have brought it along. They are very light weight, collapsible and you can stick them in your backpack and never know the difference. Find a

125

sporty one that makes you look like you just do so much hiking in the mountains that you couldn't live without it!

Walking will of course be the order of the day, every day. If you plan things right, that is. In lots of very interesting and affordable countries you can take taxis or public transportation for pennies. Like my beloved tuk tuks in Guatemala that would take me anywhere in town for about 75 cents. In some parts of Java and many other places in Asia the human powered bicycle rickshaws are everywhere. I guess they are considered so cool that now you can ride in them in San Diego, California and other tourist places. Trouble is a quick ride of a mile through the Gaslight District of San Diego will cost enough money to pay all your expenses for a whole day, including sleeping accommodations, in many other more colorful and exotic places. So sad that getting pulled around in a bicycle powered rickshaw in the USofA is what I would consider, in my income bracket, to be cost prohibitive and a silly luxury. Whereas in say, Indonesia, it's just a practical way to get around.

Even in exotic destinations, when you do the math and want to hang out in a place for as long as possible, you might also consider that for the cost of a couple of tuk tuk or cheap taxi rides you could walk wherever you are going and maybe have breakfast instead. Might as well walk if at all possible, and it's so healthy anyway.

There are lots of other advantages and benefits in strolling instead of riding in some motorized or humanized vehicle. In cozy little villages, things tend to not be all that scattered about as they are in even small cities in the USA. While strolling around in an exotic village you are certain to run into familiar locals in the streets or at your favorite café. Or, while out for a stroll, you might happen upon fellow travelers from even your very own country who have become your chums along the way. And off for a snack or a drink you go. This kind of pastime can truly become far more wonderful a way to spend your time than jumping into a bus or taxi, or even a tuk tuk, just to avoid the walk that you really needed anyway.

If you simply declare that you intend to make lots of exercise an important aspect of your travels, an abundance of it will await you just as you go about your normal, everyday life.

IMPROVED HEALTH. Well, so far we've got you feeling pretty good, don't we? We've pumped your self esteem and confidence. You are now a person with permission to have lots of fun and with all those great qualities you've garnered, simply everybody you meet wants to hang out with you. So love and companionship are abounding more and more every day. The folks back home, who you are keeping posted via email about all the fun and thrills you're having are green with envy and thinking you are just the neighborhood hotshot. All that respect and not to mention the endorphins surging through your body from all the walking, stair stepping and weight lifting. Need I say more about improved health?

LONGER LIFE. There are sure a lot of theories on longevity, aren't there? Some say it's genetic. That theory might be correct. Or that might be correct for some and not for others. Some studies have discovered that people who live to be more than 100 years old have three major things in common. Those things are:

> **THE ABILITY TO LET GO OF THINGS AND PEOPLE. The studies reveal that people who live to be over 100 are able to let go of things and people. If you think about it, 100 years is a long time for a person to live. But people really do live that long.**

127

Which means that those special folks who pull off this amazing feat are going see a lot of their friends and family pass on before they do. Being able to lose people and not lose yourself in the process, requires a particular mental attitude that not everyone has. However, for the sake of longevity, if that's something you want, it might be an attitude worth developing. I do believe that such an attitude is acquired (deliberately) as opposed to being just an innate quality of character. I doubt that it comes to a person as a blessing at birth so it is going to be something you will have to work at. An idea to think about and nurture. Much more on "letting go" in upcoming chapters.

A POSITIVE ATTITUDE. It seems that maintaining a positive mental attitude, corny as I realize it sounds, it essential to living more than 100 years. Doesn't it only stand to reason that a cheerful person who sees the bright and positive side of things is going to be healthier and have more reasons to WANT to live longer? Not to mention that a positive attitude is vastly superior for achieving optimum health than is a negative attitude. It seems silly to even mention anything so obvious. But then one might wonder if a positive attitude is so well know to contribute to longevity, why are so many grumpy senior citizens complaining about their health. Perhaps because they are also busy complaining about everything? Maybe figuring out ways to cheer up would be the best possible medicine.

A PASSIONATE INTEREST IN SOMETHING. According to the research, it doesn't seem to matter what that "something" might be. As long as one has a passionate interest in something, this will be another factor contributing to longevity. I suppose it could be building ships in bottles or playing canasta or learning Greek. From my perspective it could be a passionate interest in traveling or even just talking about and/or writing about travel. Only thing for sure is we are not likely to make it to 100 if we become jaded and apathetic. Something's got to turn us on to keep us alive.

Seems to me that this wild idea of seeing the world while we still have the chance is in perfect harmony with what it takes to live a very long, healthy and happy life.

FOUR
What You DO NOT Need

"He who would travel happily,
must travel light."

-Antoine de Saint-Exupery

It's possible that, since it's essential to travel light, what you do not take with you while traveling is far more important than what you take. We'll get to what you might want to take later. First here's a brief rundown about what you don't need for your travels in order to still have wonderful adventures. Maybe even more fun, the less you bring along.

The following is, for the most part, not about packing your backpack lightly. It is mostly about what NOT to pack in your head. While the physical world is discussed here, what's in your backpack, as long as it's not too much, is so minor compared to what's in your head. THAT is of paramount importance! Here's a little of both practical and mental packing, or, rather, *un*packing ideas.

A NEGATIVE ATTITUDE.

If you reject the food, ignore the customs,
fear the religion and avoid the people,
you might better stay at home.

James A. Michener

Leaving negativity at home is the single most important recommendation I or anyone can make about traveling. It is the most important thing for you to not take with you. Would that we could abandon negativity in every area of our lives. But it especially something to leave behind when traveling.

I could summarize this entire book in a couple of sentences:

1) No matter what - go travel.

2) Don't go if you generally have a negative attitude.

Does that sound too simplistic? Once again, it really is the absolute most important thing about the entire matter of traveling. In fact, Chapter 6 is about nothing BUT attitude and especially negativity. If you can't keep negativity out of your head, your backpack, your conversation, your pockets, then my bottom line advice is just simply do not go. The universe has a magical way of manifesting positive and negative thoughts. If you take them with you, expect the universe to manifest exactly what you brought/thought. Good or bad.

AN IRA. If you have an IRA, grand! You are ahead of so many of us near boomer boys and girls. But if you don't have one, it's not the end of life as we know it. So keep the worry about it OUT of your thoughts. What's needed now, more than bushels of money, are courage, creativity, open mindedness, flexibility, desire, sense of humor, positive attitude, etc. If we play our cards right, we should be able to get to and hang out in "some" other countries on just what our Uncle Sam sends our way each month. Impossible you say? Well remember the old saying, "Whether you say you can or you say you can't, you're probably right." Try to keep in mind how "WE" are the masters of our destinies!

A COLLEGE DEGREE. This is no time to worry about how smart or educated we are. All that stuff is not something to be concerned about anymore unless you are going for a senior citizen college degree, in which case you probably won't have time for travel right now anyway and I applaud you for your fabulous goals. My mother began attending the local community college when she was over 70. She was thrilled about it and

132

loved every minute of all her classes. AND she loved hanging out with the "kids." She attended for several years as an honor student.

No matter what your previous education and career and how well prepared you might have been for it, now it is simply time for you to have fun and enjoy the planet. You've earned it no matter what you've been doing.

The education you will acquire by trotting around the globe will, no doubt, far surpass any that you got in the halls of ivy anyway. By the time you've mastered the concept of "travel" (again, as opposed to vacationing) you will have your PhD in wanderlust and that's plenty fine.

AN EXTENSIVE WARDROBE. When thinking about packing a backpack, an extensive wardrobe could be highly detrimental to your effectiveness as a flexible traveler. The clothes department will, ultimately, be one of those grand experiences of "lightening up" that the entire process of taking off will bring your way. Might as well start thinking now about what you really, truly need in the way of clothing. For example, why would you need more than one jacket? How many pairs of pants do you really wear in your at-home life anyway? Did you know that no matter what affordable country you go to there are people who will do your laundry for peanuts and have it back to you, often ironed, within hours or anyway the next day.

More surprises about wardrobe. In the truly affordable countries there are tailors who will make just about anything you might need or want to wear. And not only that, they will provide you with "custom made" for just a few dollars.

Believe it or not there are even thrift stores in other countries. Recently I was in a small town in Costa Rica that had a thrift store on almost every block!

Here's a thought from my Mom who did not promote fun but had tons of great, practical ideas. She used to love to say, "This isn't a fashion show!" We are travelers after all. We going to "see what we can see" and "be" where we are going to be, right? Or are "we going to all the trouble and expense of travel in order to be seen?" I think not.

It can't hurt to start thinking very soon about what you will want in the way of clothes *you do not* really need to take. Again, even if you never go anywhere, the exercise in pondering what you "really" need to survive this life and what is superfluous will be invaluable.

THE PERMISSION OF YOUR FRIENDS AND FAMILY. Do you think I'm kidding? Let's say you never made noise that sounded like you were thinking of taking off to parts unknown. Then suddenly (maybe after reading this book) you do start making those kinds of noises. You might be amazed at what "they" have to say.

Your kids might really shock you and tell you how thrilled they are with your plans. "What have you been waiting for Mom?" You might wonder if they are trying to hurry along their inheritance, if such a thing exists at all in their futures. Truth is our offspring are not a bit anxious to think about their parents sitting around and withering to death. The kids might totally surprise you and press you right into action. But let's be realistic. Parents are already heroes in the eyes of their children. For your kids, you will only become more of a hero for even thinking about taking off on a bold adventure.

134

How about your friends and peers? Well that's another story entirely. In this case you might encounter some spoken or worse yet, unspoken envy. You are almost assured of hearing from your friends, amazing tales of the horrors of travel. The tales will be as dramatic and blood chilling as anything you've seen on TV - in the suspense movies. For even more impact your friends can pull this scary information right off the official travel advisories on the World Wide Web. Beyond the official news stories, they will range from such things as, "My third cousin got Montezuma's Revenge in Acapulco and didn't recover for a whole year." All the way to kidnappings and murders in Central American countries and/or more exotic places like the Philippine Islands. It's not like all that stuff doesn't happen. Reports of such events can be found on the World Wide Web for just about any country you might choose. But your friends will rarely go into much detail about how much of that sort of thing is happening within 100 miles of where you (and they) already live.

You are almost certain to hear tales that would make any sane person take pause and reconsider the whole adventure. Try to keep in mind how over-dramatized incidents in your own neighborhood appear to friends on the other side of the country. For example, I lived in the San Fernando Valley in California. Pretty tame for the most part. However, there are frequent brush fires in the neighborhood where I lived and if one should occur anywhere in Southern California, friends and family will call in a panic presuming that everything, including me, has gone up in smoke. Yet the real action might be 200 or 300 miles away – or more! I suppose it's just human nature to look for things to become alarmed about.

A TRAVELING COMPANION. You may find that reaching out to strangers, while possibly uncomfortable until you get the hang of it, is easier when you don't have the safety of continually chatting with your regular traveling companion.   You are much less likely to get the rich benefits out of traveling if you don't deliberately put yourself in situations where *you must* interact with local people or other travelers who are sharing similar challenges.   If you take along a traveling companion you will naturally encounter fewer reasons to step out of your comfort zone as that person will naturally become a sort of security blanket.   As I said elsewhere in this book, it is almost impossible to spend much time alone when travelling. Maybe one of the reasons travel is so rewarding is not so much what you "see" but more who you encounter.   It's my personal opinion that you would have to go out of your way to avoid meeting new, fun and interesting friends every day, all day.   Well, that is if you are "out there" and not holed up in your room.

A VACATIONERS MENTALITY.   I must make the distinction again between travelers and "tourists" or "vacationers" because I am not promoting "vacationing."   Vacationing is an entirely different happening than traveling.   What I am proposing in this book is that you become a "traveler."

A traveler has somehow arranged his or her life to enable wandering the planet for extended periods of time.   Sometimes even wandering aimlessly for undetermined periods of time.   Oooooh what a treat!

Some fortunate travelers have the financial means to go and do whatever they wish and in any style they choose.   Well, we can't really call them fortunate, can we?   It surely is not luck for well heeled people, in most cases, because they planned very, very carefully, indeed!   But even the well-heeled traveler may still decide to take the shoestring path, which is what this book is all about.   They may choose that path because traveling on a shoestring can actually be more fun than the five star style in so many ways.

136

Or perhaps some of the well-heeled amassed their fortunes being frugal in the first place. And, they see no reason to suddenly start throwing away money for no reason at all - ever. Wishing to continue to be frugal, if that's your nature anyway, can be an excellent motivation for shoestring travel.

Tourists and/or vacationers are off for a specific period of time. Their intentions are to either gaze at stuff a lot, learn a lot, rest a lot or play a lot. All within a relatively short period of time. More often than not, vacationers/tourists are following a fairly, or extremely structured agenda. Usually vacationers/tourists are off for one week to a month. These are all wonderful objectives but slightly different from the loose agenda (or lack of agenda) of the "traveler." Think more of being a wanderer or perhaps a vagabond.

The traveler is a weird duck who must, somewhat compulsively, inhale all they can of everything on Earth to which they can expose themselves in their lifetime, no matter what it takes or costs. There is a certain passion and compulsion in the "traveler" that makes him or her quite a bold and unique character. When you travel WITHOUT a companion, these are the strange sort of people you are more likely to interact with. Other travelers, that is – other bold and adventurous folks.

If you are reading this book for guidance about traveling for extended periods of time on a limited income and you have all the time in the world, then welcome to the exciting world of the "traveler!" Your adventures will leave those of the tourist and vacationer looking quite pale and dull by comparison.

BIGOTRY.

"Travel is fatal to prejudice, bigotry, and narrow-mindedness."

- MARK TWAIN

I must confess that both my parents were bigots. I think it was the style in their day and bigotry was quite commonly accepted in their social circles. They knew they were bigots, had not a bit of concern about it and besides they have gone to heaven by now. So I suppose it's OK to tell you about it now. I didn't approve of their bigotry but then I did notice that my parents never actually look for my approval. Did anyone's?

To me, even as a small child, bigotry always seemed quite dumb. Martin Luther King, Jr., said, *"I have a <u>dream</u> that my four little children will one day live in a nation where they will not be judged by the color of their skin, but by **the content of their character.**"*

I'm sticking with that concept. And I'm thinking a person would have a lot more fun and a far more enriching experience traveling if he or she could leave all thought of one color, race, culture, etc., being any better or worse than another. If we travel to learn, how can we expect to learn anything if we start out with preconceived notions and closed minds? I think they call that prejudice, right? So try to leave behind cultural or racial discrimination, as they will only close one's mind and limit one's possibilities for a truly enriching, expansive and thrilling experience.

AN AUTOMOBILE. Now I ask you, how can you scrunch an automobile into your backpack? Of course, for traveling to most countries you probably won't have much choice about taking your car or not because it just won't be possible or it might just be highly impractical. Many people I suppose could plan some long road trip activities. That would more likely be jaunts through the USofA. At least for the message of this writing, I am more inclined to support *leaving* the country to experience the richness of other cultures than exploring the UsofA if that is your country of origin. Although I realize that we do in the USofA have almost as many cultures as we have states. I'm not a traitor or against seeing the USA in your Chevrolet. It's just that what this book happens to be about is foreign travel.

This may just be my personal preference but it would seem to me that having a vehicle along on an international jaunt would limit your opportunities to experience the full spectrum of travel experiences. Wouldn't it also be a kind of burden to have to worry about parking, gasing up, repairs, insurance (even more tricky in foreign lands), not to mention worrying if anything should happen (your fault or not) that it might result in your spending the rest of your days in some dark and stinking foreign prison? Things like that do happen in foreign lands. I'm thinking, "Not worth it".

Much of the fun of interacting with fellow travelers happens when you encounter them on public transportation or even simply walking down the street. Taking a car along would be somewhat like taking a travel companion. In many ways it might simplify the experience and provide a kind of safe harbor. Maybe taking a vehicle would make it more comfortable in some ways. But in other ways it might eliminate much of the color, excitement and wonder of an adventure. And what if you took a vehicle you kind of liked and it had a hopeless breakdown in the middle of some desert in Mexico? Could you bear to just abandon it and carry on with your good time or would that seem a bit too cold? Might it's becoming inoperable perhaps require you to completely change your entire agenda?

And might such an unfortunate happening eat up your "fun" funds and "fun" time?

The best way to discover for yourself what you do not need to bring along when traveling for extended periods is to venture off on the first trip and truly experience the nuisance of lugging things you discover you could easily have done without.

FIVE
Take Me Along With You

Of all the good information in Chapter 4 about what you don't need to take with you when you decide to fly away into the unknown, there are only a very few material things that you **must** take that will not weigh anything at all. Like, for example, your passport. But not to worry. That little detail is under an ounce.

To enjoy a truly wonderful, fun, memorable trip – be it one month or three years – what you will mostly need to take along with you are things that will all fit right between your ears.

A POSITIVE ATTITUDE. Well, there it is again - the other side of negativity. There is that corny, overdone, over emphasized and "we're getting so tired of hearing about it" concept: POSITIVE MENTAL ATTITUDE. And once again I refer you to Chapter 6 for more badgering about how important a positive attitude really is. If you can't take it (a positive attitude that is), don't go.

YOUR PASSPORT. Yes, you will need a passport if you plan to leave the country and if you don't already have one it's never too late to get one. You can do it online if you are computer savvy, which I highly recommend you become before leaving. Or you can simply go to the post office, fill out a form, bring some good ID, ideally a birth certificate, hand over some money, get your picture taken and within a month or so the world will become your oyster. So, why not get started early on this? It only costs around $100 which seems a small price to pay for turning an entire planet into an oyster. Even just having a passport is pretty neat. Just think, if you don't have one you cannot leave the country. I just hate the idea of being

141

told I can't do something. Especially something as liberating as being free to go wherever I want to go – in the whole world.

DETACHMENT. To have a really great time, unencumbered by all the stuff back home, it's important to have and take along a **willingness to detach.** By detach I mean detaching from possessions and (don't take this part too hard), you will need to detach from people also, to some extent. That does not mean that you become cold blooded, heartless and no longer love and adore your friends and family. Nor does it mean that you won't miss them while you are away. It is merely an attitude of *willingness* to allow the people you love to take care of themselves while you go off and enjoy YOURSELF for a while. Remember the part about how it's your turn?

Imagine if all those adventurous guys of olden days had been unwilling to detach from their loved ones for the last many thousands of years. The United States would not even exist because it would never have been discovered, explored, settled and, ultimately it would never have become the amazing country it is today. People took off in ships with essentially no communications whatsoever. They had no idea if they would ever see their friends and families again and very often they didn't. Columbus didn't get to Skype his Mom to let her know he was doing OK in the new land he ran into. Do you think we maybe have gotten soft?

Detaching from your stuff (your material possessions) is a bit simpler although almost impossible for a great many people. For more detailed inspiration on detaching from material possession, refer to Chapter 9 on Homelessness. While homelessness is the ultimate detachment from one's material possessions, it will certainly not be necessary for everyone who wishes to see the world. Many solutions exist for temporarily putting your home on hold so you can see the world less encumbered. Many less drastic means exist to help you get out the door. Things such as (excuse what I realize is dirty words for many) reverse mortgages, renting out your home and house swapping, etc.

A SENSE OF HUMOR. In my experience it is pretty rare to run into travelers who do not have a good sense of humor. This could be because they are having so much fun out there, doing exactly as they please, that they are usually happy and in a pretty good mood. Who wouldn't be – doing exactly as you please? So maybe there isn't even a need to talk about taking a good sense of humor along in your travels because you might just discover you can acquire one on the travel trail if you didn't have one when you left.

I should say, however, that it can't hurt one bit to start out with a sense of humor and take it with you because you are definitely going to need it immediately - before you get out of the USofA. Personally, I'm sort of inclined to laugh at almost everything. But maybe that's just me. Things that will make a lot of people crazy and exasperated will frequently make me laugh instead. If one has a choice between laughing or grumbling, wouldn't you pick laughter any day? I sure would. Laughter is so much better for your health that a lot of dreary negative feelings. So try to arrange your mind to see humor in everything if you possibly can. For example. . . .

In the old days they wanted us to arrive at the airport an hour ahead of our flight and we grumbled about the inconvenience. I left the USofA a couple of months before I started this book, way back in 2008 (actually December 31, 2007 as I was in the air at midnight – which got me a cheaper flight). Back then they wanted us to be two hours early. While in Costa Rica in 2010 for almost three months, some new potential terrorist thing happened

143

and they were then asking passengers to arrive THREE hours ahead of their flights. Are they kidding? Must be, so I just have to laugh. So if I'm sitting in an airport or on a beach with a good book what's the difference? Don't forget – no matter where you go, there you are!

In the old days when you used to want to go somewhere and flying was the best mode of travel, there was a plane to take you there, directly. Now it takes two or three planes and you may first have to cross the entire country just to go a few hours due South of where you started. Unless you are in Canada, that is. I was amazed to learn that Candians can travel round trip, **direct** to Costa Rica for as little as $350. Bet you even get lunch on that flight! Go figure! Maybe airlines that fly out of Canada are just more sensible. None of it makes any sense to me so what do I do? I laugh.

Back when there was a direct flight to just about anywhere, there was usually also a good meal waiting up there in the sky for you. Now it's "your guess is as good as mine." And back in the friendly skies it used to be a sweet stewardess would happily bring you whatever you needed. These days you will be embarrassed to ask for much of anything, lest you are dealt a dirty look for daring to do such a thing. What ever happened to little bags of peanuts and big sweet smiles? I miss those.

If all that air travel jazz isn't enough to make you burst into peals of laughter – take off your shoes. That ought to do it! God forbid you don't put your shoes through the x-ray machine. They must check every single pair of shoes because you might have a bomb in your heel.

The world of travel is chock full of aggravations from the minute you step into the airport. Many are understandable. But so many more just make me want to scratch my head and ask myself if there is a conspiracy underway to keep us Yanks from leaving the country at all.

There is some hope, however. You can always have a pre-flight cocktail. You can barely bring your shampoo on your flight so forget sneaking a bottle of cheap booze on board to slip into your complimentary OJ and bolster your courage if you suffer fear of flying. But just think, you can pause at the bar in the airport and have a $13 martini. Don't have two though because you could frolic through one entire day of foreign travel (your hotel and meals) just by not spending what it would have cost you for two martinis at the airport in the USofA.

If you aren't laughing yet, maybe you had better be very conscious and deliberate about bringing your sense of humor the minute you leave home because at least for the first part of your trip you are really going to need it.

SOME COMPUTER SAVVY. Chapter 7 – Get Smart and Get Going, provides great detail on the importance of letting computer technology into your life before you pack your bags. This is very important because it will serve you from the very beginning in even deciding where you want to go and why. It can even help you get your passport, find hostels and hotels, buy tickets, get maps, buy supplies, keep in touch, etc. In today's world, while it is not impossible to travel as a technology ostrich (with your head in the sand) it would make your challenge far more complex than it would be if you choose to jump on the high tech wagon with your head held high and out of the sand!

A CURSORY KNOWLEDGE OF WEB BROWSING. Until you have experienced the magic of exploring the entire world by surfing the web, you cannot fully understand how hugely beneficial it will be for you to explore places, maps, tickets, hotels, hostels, parks, special events, weather and updates of all kinds. The list of benefits is endless. A great way to find out first hand what I'm talking about (if you are not already computer savvy) is to think of an imaginary trip you would like to take and go enlist the help of a grandchild or other young person to sit down and show you how much you can learn in minutes about your fantasy destination.

AT LEAST A CURSORY KNOWLEDGE OF EMAIL. Again I urge you to take Chapter 7 very seriously because even this one small aspect of understanding computers will allow you to be in constant contact with the people you love. Your loved ones will be so happy to hear from you and getting the latest news from home can bring an amazing peace to your travels that might not exist if you were traversing some exotic country worrying about everybody back home with minimal communication.

Sometimes, when I am out of the country, I will receive a one line email from my daughter, who lives in a very remote cabin in the Sequoias (the same one where I got snowed in) where internet (at her end) is pretty unreliable much of the time. One line from her saying anything at all is often the most important thing to happen to me for days. Talk about make my day!

I have concluded that I am not so awfully courageous in my world wanderings. I have just discovered that by fully embracing technology the world has shrunk down to a size that I can manage. What once was "far away" is no longer far at all. I must attribute that to all the conveniences that are now available for us so we can be connected with our loved ones on a daily basis.

ENOUGH GOOD HEALTH TO HEFT YOUR OWN BAGS. It is rather essential that you are able to manage your own luggage pretty much most of the time. Although you will frequently hear in this book reference to a "backpack," I do not necessarily propose that you do the kind of backpacking where you lug along a tent, cooking utensils, a stove, sleeping bag, etc. - unless you like that type of travel, of course. Then go for it! I refer to a backpack only because in many situations it is far better and easier to carry a backpack and walk over uneven paths, and/or up and down hills and stairs with a backpack, than it is to pull a suitcase. I have done both and each has its own advantages and inconveniences. In truth and for my own personal preferences, I am more inclined to carry my backpack to a nice clean hostel, hotel or bungalow where I can stay for several weeks and get to feel really close to the local color and culture. While I love to travel and see new things, I don't personally like to see new things every few days as do many, many travelers who travel to "see" rather than to "be." More on these concepts in Chapter 13 – How Long is Long Enough?

GOOD ENOUGH HEALTH TO GET ON AND OFF BUSES. Many travelers, even many young ones, are very put off by the thought of taking buses in strange lands. They opt instead for tourist shuttles which can be relatively expensive. In many countries buses might be a bad idea and again, the importance of being able to do serious research on the World Wide Web can be invaluable in this regard. But in countries that have excellent bus systems it is simply unnecessary to take tourist shuttles much of the time. The difference in cost can make it very important to give careful consideration to opting for the bus. To utilize buses in countries where they are practical, it's important to be in good enough health to pull yourself and your bags onto a bus.

Again, I personally don't care for the lugging, pulling, pushing and generally uncomfortable aspects of travel and I avoid doing it frequently as

I prefer to get to a place and, if I like it, and then stay put for as long as I can.

As an example of a cost comparison I recently traveled from a city near the San Jose airport in Costa Rica to a beach that I discovered I loved. I made the trip twice as a friend arrived from California and I returned from the beach to the airport to pick her up when she arrived. Then I needed to get us both back to my favorite beach. The buses in Costa Rica are pretty wonderful. For long distances (around 5 hours) the buses are very large, generally air conditioned, have comfortable seats and the drivers are cautious and professional, taking few chances, unlike bus drivers in many other Central American countries. Between the two of us we made a total of six one way trips (2 round trips for me and one for my friend). Each trip cost about $7.00 on the bus or a total of $42 for all 6 trips. The same travel on tourist shuttles would have been about $40 for each trip (per person) or a total of $240 for all six trips. My lightening quick mind tells me we saved almost $200 in bus fare alone, which paid for almost all our food for the entire week that my friend vacationed with me at the beach. This resulted in great cost savings and only took maybe an hour longer than the shuttles. Shuttle rides are far more hair raising and there is much less room in the seats. So are they better? Or is it just an illusion that they are better?

My point in describing the advantages of the bus transport relates to the importance of being sure one is healthy and strong enough to climb into the bus with one's own bags. Not to say that no one would be willing to help. However, in many cases where everyone who is getting on a bus is dealing with their own bags, it is a good idea to be prepared to be as independent as possible.

GOOD ENOUGH HEALTH TO WALK AND CLIMB STAIRS. One thing I must compliment the great USofA for is how much effort has been put into making so many things handicapped friendly. This is not typically true in the sort of third world countries where one can afford to travel on a shoestring. Because of my personal preference for traveling a little bit and staying a long while, stairs have become less of a problem for me.

When I arrive in a town where, after extensive research on the WWW and a short in person review, I would like to stay for a month or more, I initially take whatever accommodations are available at the least expense, knowing that, unless the place is perfect, it will be temporary. To be honest, the good fortune of finding the perfect accommodations immediately is rare, even if one reserves ahead of time on the internet. Once in Bali I shopped through six different homestays until I found one that made me completely happy. So I barely unpack until I find "my place."

My very next order of business the day after I arrive in a town is to go shopping for the most ideal home for my needs. Although stairs are not a particular problem for me "yet," I don't especially care for them as a routine part of my life. I feel they just add an extra thing to trip on and cut my fun time short. I try to be very careful NOT to do that. Why make things harder than they need to be? There just is no need to go out of my way to deal with stairs if it is not absolutely necessary.

While there are such actions as explained above that one can take to minimize stairs as a daily routine, one must be prepared for stairs and know that many, many times they simply cannot be avoided. It is, therefore, essential that the traveler be in good enough health to be able to negotiate unexpected stairways and again, perhaps negotiate the stairways while also being responsible for one's bags.

In order to have the freedom to become comfortable with wherever it is you happen to be visiting, nothing serves as well as the good old fashioned stroll through town. But truly there is no reason that a person need do any more walking when traveling than he or she would if they stayed home. My idea of a good time is to locate a place to stay that is clean, inexpensive and comfortable and also near all the things I like to do and places I like to eat. If I really like the town why shouldn't I stay for a month or more? If I don't like it, as happens many times, I'll move on to another one that I do like.

For example, I had occasion to stay in a relatively small village called Panajachel on Lake Atitlan in Guatemala. The places I found to settle in were downstairs and walking distance to wherever I might have wanted to go in the entire village. During the day I walked everywhere. I would visit internet cafe's, shop, visit with new friends, sit by the lake and read, see a movie at a special bar where movies are part of the service, visit the health club or whatever suited my fancy. Sometimes, however, I would stay too long with friends and want to go home after dark. While the neighborhood was perfectly safe and I felt it was very free of crooks and bad guys, walking in the dark is not always as safe because the surfaces of the sidewalks can be rather uneven and perhaps not as safe as they might be in the light of day when one could see the pitfalls. So my routine was to walk everywhere all day and if I ended my day far from home and it was dark, take a tuk tuk back to my hotel for under 75 cents. If I did that every single day for a whole month my expense would still only be under $23. Insurance for my car back in California costs more than that before it even rolls out the driveway. And that is before registration, gas, service and repairs, etc.

My point is that it's pretty cheap to keep yourself safe so why take unnecessary chances.

SIX
How Full is Your Glass

The marvelous richness of human experience would lose something of rewarding joy if there were no limitations to overcome. The hilltop hour would not be half so wonderful if there were no dark valleys to traverse.

- Helen Keller

Before you ever even think about packing your suitcase, or better yet your backpack, consider the packing or repacking of your outlook on life, as needed.

Everything you ever heard or read about a positive attitude has just become the most important guidance you have ever gotten and the most important single thing you will want to take on your adventures.

There truly is magic and power in a positive attitude. You will treasure the power of it when one day you trip on a rock in a village in some remote third world paradise and *don't* fall on your face and break something but instead, miraculously regain your balance.

Maybe we can borrow the second step from the twelve steps of Alcoholics Anonymous for this. Something like:

We came to believe that a power greater than ourselves could keep us from breaking a bone!

This book is hardly a lecture on twelve step stuff or a dispute on whether or not God exists. It is, however, a reminder that we create our own reality every minute we're alive, in harmony with the magic of the universe. The success of our adventure depends entirely on the attitude we maintain throughout.

By the time one reaches the age of the BIG THANK YOU (retirement), one should surely have encountered endless experiences of the power of positive thinking.

You may even want to take some time to examine proof from your own life. Recall the time in your life when everything seemed to work flawlessly – even miraculously. It would be quite inconsistent with the laws of the universe if you had been convinced during those times that life sucked and nothing ever turns out the way you want – and then, contrary to your negative attitude, it did turn out great.

We all know that life simply does not work that way. There are so many books on the subject that I'm not even going to go there.

The most important thing is this. It is essential you take a positive attitude on your adventure.

If you just naturally believe the glass is half full you shouldn't have too much work to do before your plane takes off. On the other hand, if things just don't seem to ever work out for you and you have no desire to examine the way you (yourself) approach life (how YOU call the shots) and no desire to turn your attitude around in a very major way if it isn't already fully positive – DON'T LEAVE HOME - PLEASE.

Recall the age old theory that if you say you *can* or you say you *can't*, you're right! You are the boss!

There are a million challenges to your well-being when you decide to embark on any adventure. Even say something as mundane as eating steak (you know you could choke to death don't you?) or going to the market (slip on slime in the aisle). Absolutely there are many more possibilities for illness and mishaps in a third world country or other exotic foreign lands. But your attitudes and beliefs are still the controlling factor. Most people strongly believe they will make it to and from the market unscathed by misfortune. So they usually do. If one believed she could wander through, say, Thailand without mishap, there is a very excellent likelihood that her happy journey would happen as well.

I am not suggesting you cast all caution to the wind and take your aging body into a jungle without a guide. I am suggesting that you exercise the utmost caution. But hold strongly to the belief that you will, if you choose, arrive back in your native country and homeland none the worse for having adventured off to exotic lands. I am suggesting that you can experience places most of your peers will never have the courage to experience if you make sure to take a positive attitude along as your most valuable asset.

Speaking of courage, are you wondering if you have the courage to embark on adventures to far away places that might be dangerous and on top of that do you have what it takes to take on this challenge with limited funds? What about fear and courage and positive attitude relative to dollars and traveling alone?

All I know for sure is that I have lived through everything I write about in this book all by myself. I am not sharing theories with you. Only my own first hand experiences. Throughout my adventures I was continuously examining what there was about **myself** that made it possible for me to find and go to the next ashram, book the next flight, wander off to the next unknown village – all without a traveling companion for security and a huge pile of money in my pocket or at home.

In the beginning I pondered such words as "fear" and "courage" and truly questioned my sanity on a few ferries and "chicken" buses. Now, many, many months into this exploration, I have come to understand that a positive attitude is essential when encountering such words as "fear" and "courage" and when facing those situations that bring on those feelings.

There is an incredible power and magic in having a positive attitude - in truly believing in the goodness of people in general and the power of the universe to take care of your needs. There is power in trusting that if you remain truly and totally positive, even events that appear negative will ultimately prove to be the best possible things that could have happened. Polyanna maybe. Effective? Definitely yes!

It is not always easy to examine your own attitude. But keep in mind that if you believe people always get the runs in foreign lands you will almost certainly become inhabited by exotic and destructive amoebas. If, on the other hand, you believe that you can, through the sheer power of your will and positive attitude, defy the law of averages, then you can. And, to that end, you will be the person who is most inclined to be cautious and most likely to investigate and employ strategies to create a body that does not become host to strange foreign visitors or mishaps.

Certainly DO NOT throw /*caution to the wind. But don't practice your cautious behavior while shivering in terror. Consider caution a practicality – not a cure for fear.

For example, if I were to tell some people they could avoid intestinal parasites and the miserable results of having such traveling companions by taking 22 drops of grapefruit seed extract at the first sign of intestinal distress, many would just ignore that information. Instead choosing to go brush their teeth in Guatemalan water straight out of the tap. In no time they could say, "See, I was right. One just gets these things in foreign lands. I knew I should have stayed home!"

In my humble opinion, it isn't worth suffering with foreign microbes just to have the glory of being "right."

And how is this swallowing bad bacteria "being right" about attitude you might wonder.

We are sure to act in ways consistent with what we say is so. Suppose I say life sucks and it is not safe in other countries and, therefore, it's more prudent to stay home. Then it is by all means in my best interests to stay in the great USofA, kick back, watch soaps and CNN or whatever. On the other hand, I can say that life is one never ending opportunity for fun and joy and that I have the knowledge and intention to keep well, wherever I go. If I say that instead I will be free to travel about the planet because I will be sure to exercise care in all I do and I will encounter miracles all along the way.

If I pack my positive attitude together with an intelligent, well informed plan and a small bag of natural remedies and prophylactics to ward off things like microbes and flying and crawling bugs, then I am, in the end, certain to remain healthy and have a wonderful adventure for however long I choose to wander the planet.

Falling into fear will be to abandon your positive attitude because, what is fear anyway but doubt that good will surely come your way.

I met a man in Guatemala (let's call him Dave) from New York City, New York. I was hanging out in a sidewalk café during Easter week – a grand fiesta time in the little village where I was living. I was having a really great time with a friend who knew this fellow so he dropped by and we started to chat.

After about 10 minutes I noticed that everything this fellow had to say described one of the following: badness, sadness, wrongness or injustice. If his thoughts did not include the exact negative sentiments listed above, then his sentences would at least contain the word "but," a word carefully planted to invalidate anything he may have accidentally said that smacked of positive. I decided this fellow was sent to me by my author muses to demonstrate exactly what the opposite of a positive attitude looks like.

I was so intrigued that a person could discover so much negativity in the exact same surroundings that I had been so enjoying for the previous couple of months.

Dave was healthy, fit, lively, cheerful and even fun to talk with. The only clue to his attitude was that his "words" were filled with the woes of our little village, the woes of the entire country and, in fact, woes of all of Central America. And not only that, all those many woes extended to the sad condition of Dave's own hometown, New York City, the entire United States of America and, in fact, not to leave anything out – pretty much the entire planet. Seemed, according to Dave anyway, we are doomed. All of us.

Yet this fellow was somehow upbeat in his spirit and demeanor.

When I could no longer bear the suspense for one more moment I asked Dave straight out something that might have seemed a silly question except that Dave was so upbeat I wasn't really sure. I simply asked, "Dave, are you happy?"

He proudly and cheerfully announced, "Oh no! I'm not a happy guy. How can I be happy with all these terrible things going on?"

It was almost as if this fellow was happy about not being a happy person and, even more bizarre he seemed downright proud of his state of "not happy." The more we talked, the more clear it became that Dave somehow felt it was his duty as a caring and humane human being to NOT be happy in the face of a planet overflowing with miseries and woes. He had it somehow wired that by being not happy he was being good. A decent human being.

It also became clear that Dave (almost 60 years old) was intent on holding on to his goodness, which he manifested unfortunately as negativity, until the day he dies. He cheerfully announced that he's already planned for the day he dies because he has no intention of going through all those indignities of old age and will simply "off" himself at that point.

On my introducing into the conversation the possibility of Dave having the power to choose to be happy in the face of all that global misery, Dave's eyes sort of glazed over and he became mute. Finally, after a rather long pause of shock and speechlessness, Dave declared such a concept to be an impossibility and completely out of the question.

Clearly, Dave's most significant paradigm is "life sucks!" Yet, in spite of his thoughts, he obviously finds life entertaining. Dave presented me with a most fascinating demonstration of all the multifaceted aspects of negativity.

Just a reminder. This is not a self-help book or a book on psychology. A psychological healing I'm told takes at least five years, thousands of dollars and hours. I was always so amused back in the days of the Schick centers when they would imply you could recover from alcohol or cigarette addiction with a two week program and a couple of two day follow ups.

In reality, count on five years of hard work in a mental health recovery program if we're lucky and dedicated. It's time consuming and expensive to unravel our hangups. I hope we have already established that we don't have the time or the money right now for that kind of exercise. Maybe we can perk up our positive mental attitudes with an epiphany or two instead of the five year route which we certainly cannot spare the time for just now!

This book, rather than being about how to be happy, is about enjoying what few years are left to us retirees. Good news is that truly and fully enjoying your retirement might just make you very happy. Given that time and financial prudence are of the essence, I am not going to suggest that before you pack your one lightweight bag you go off and spend five years and a couple of two day follow ups in psychotherapy.

What I am going to propose, if you should notice that your thoughts seem to align with Dave's, is a paradigm shift in your *decisions* about life. It will be lots cheaper and easier and then you can go travel a little (actually alot) more safely.

Change your mind. Decide you can be happy, even in the face of a doomed planet and all the lesser evils that abound everywhere. Maybe do it like the twelve step people. One day at a time. Just live for "now." Declare yourself happy. It can be done and right now we don't have time to drag the process out too much.

If your attitude is positive, then you are part of the solution. If you allow yourself to maintain a negative attitude, then you are part of the problem. It's just that simple. And this is true not only of the minor stuff of life, like

158

your own health, for example. This is true for the grand and global picture as well.

There is nothing good or right or decent or wonderful about unhappiness or negativity. There will be no reward in heaven if you decline the option (and it is an option) to be a happy camper. There may be some good karma to be had or some heavenly reward for your good intentions, thoughts and deeds. But forget about getting any payback or merit badges for being unhappy or negative. The only thing you will get from that is maybe sick, lousy memories, solitude, a severe shortage of fun friends and, quite possibly, dead before your time if you choose to overindulge in negativity.

It may be true that misery loves company. But do you really want to keep company with the miserable of this world?

If you are deeply conscious of and concerned about the fact that children are starving, that we are involved in needless and deadly military conflict, that the planet's resources are being squandered and polluted, that whole species of fishes and turtles are becoming extinct, that the world economy is shaky – GOOD!

There has never been a better time in your whole life than right now for you to choose your battle and plow ahead full speed with all the gusto and positive energy you can muster to begin to address the issues that you find most compelling.

Once you hit the road and leave the country you will discover that things are even worse than you ever dreamed. Then your possibilities for making a difference in the world – before you leave this life – will increase dramatically. The hopelessness of it all might, in fact, press you to realize that little old you, single handedly, cannot even begin to scratch the surface.

Don't worry. Be happy. Take action if you will. And be happy (thrilled even) about doing it.

> *I am only one; but still I am one. I cannot do*
> *everything, but still I can do something.*
> *I will not refuse to do something I can do.*
> **Helen Keller**

You might also be surprised to discover in your travels that other retirees who have taken off to live their travel dreams are, simultaneously, attacking the world's problems, one scratch at a time. And they are also experiencing and enjoying many fascinating cultures and keeping company with some pretty wonderful folks from all around the world who are not miserable but happy to be involved and doing their part – however minor it might seem – to make the world a better place.

Negativity and unhappiness about "how things are" will rob you of the physical strength and well being to get out, see the world and at the same time chip away at the problems out there in the world that you claim are making you negative and unhappy in the first place.

For some people, being negative is just a good excuse to do nothing. Or worse, to lie around and be lethargic watching CNN and moaning, "Oh woe is me – it's all too hopeless anyway!"

OK! But just so you know, there are grey-haired seniors in exotic countries all over the world who have chosen an entirely different, more meaningful, energetic and helpful approach to the rest of their productive lives.

Why not switch off soaps and CNN and join their ranks? If you don't drown in a capsized ferry taking you off to some little village in Asia or Central America, or if you don't get kidnapped in the Philippines and held for the ransom of your huge Social Security check, then I can assure you there are better things in store for you than you can find on TV.

Your improved health is almost guaranteed and you can be pretty sure your life will also be extended from all your activity, enthusiasm and positive energy. All of which will greatly enhance your health.

SEVEN

Get Smart and Get Going

*Life is a succession of lessons
which must be lived to be understood.*

- Helen Keller

FINDING YOUR WAY. Before the World Wide Web existed, many of the concepts in this book would have been difficult to impossible. To have written a book such as this would have been a cruel form of teasing. Because finding your way to some of the places suggested would have been quite a challenge, indeed.

I say that because in this book I will not provide, in most cases, specific direction (for example names or web addresses of retreats) I have made this decision because in many cases it could be detrimental for any particular retreat to be inundated with endless applications from excited senior citizens wanting to come and wash dishes and do yoga. I would not want to cause such distress.

I offer here only concepts and leave the reader to find his or her own specific direction based on personal interest and instincts.

What I will direct the reader to is the World Wide Web. And with that direction I encourage the reader to make friends with computers in general.

I include this discussion of the World Wide Web (www) in this section because it is most definitely a timely gift that we have at our disposal now that did not exist when we were in school. Anybody remember learning to type on manual typewriters with no letters on the keys?

Begin your education as simply and cheaply as possible. At the library maybe.

Although the hours of being open have become a bit scarce lately, you will find that just about every public library in the USA will have computers for you to use – free. Free should fit into your budget perfectly no matter what your budget might be.

You might want to consider swallowing your pride and giving up grumbling about technology. You can ask your grandchildren to teach you a thing or two about "browsing the web". If you don't have a grandchild, not to worry. You could probably rent a kid pretty cheap (a twelve year old will do), or check out a book at the library for free or take a class at adult education for probably close to free or maybe even completely free.

There are only about four things to learn about browsing on the WWW anyway. The rest is a matter of using your imagination a lot. Come on. If a twelve-year old can teach you, how tough can it be? This is no time to be too proud to learn something new. Especially something as important as this.

Electronic Mail. Without the gift of electronic mail, the prospect of traveling the planet and being away from your loved ones could, indeed, be a lonely and isolating prospect. I'm not sure I would even be all that comfortable with it myself. I did do some traveling before the World Wide Web and email and I was forever walking miles in almost unbearable heat looking for public phones from which I could phone home.

Today, however, there are so many internet cafes everywhere that you can communicate with the folks back home 3 or more times a day if you want and for very little money in most cases.

If not for email, when I received the news of my son's untimely death while I was in Guatemala writing this book, I would have felt so disconnected from home, friends and family that I would have felt I had no choice but to return to California on the next plane out.

I needed support. I needed information about what had happened. I needed to give direction and authorizations. But most of all I needed to touch my family and friends and to share my grief in real time and to be supported by and feel the love of "my people."

All that and more was possible with email. The amount of phone calls that it would have taken to accomplish all that would, at that time, have been exorbitantly expensive and prohibitive for someone on a limited Social Security income.

My friends and family encouraged me to continue diligently with my book because they felt, and I agreed, that the message is important for people who don't have years and years to make a decision to travel. If not for advanced communications I probably would have abandoned this book just as it was barely getting through the "good idea" stage.

I was aware of the reality and the finality of my son's life and that there was nothing I could do in California to bring him back to us. My friends and family were doing everything needed so that I could continue this project. They sent me love via email. Via email they encouraged me. They kept me informed and picked me up when I fell. Via email they did everything but hug me. But when I needed a hug I would simply go to an internet café and there I would inevitably find 2 or 3 emails from home, filled with love, hugs and encouragement to continue writing.

Through emails, my friends and family kept me remembering that this book is truly about "living" even as I was dealing with the pains of facing "death" in the worse possible way. They reminded me of the importance of not letting time slip away from us because there really isn't much certainty about life for any of us.

Technology is not something to resent and resist. It can truly be our best friend and it is one friendship well worth cultivating.

VOIP – VOICE OVER INTERNET TELEPHONING – What is this thing called Skype? I can hardly believe the wonders of Skype myself and have spent many, many years deeply involved in high tech systems and even large telephone systems. When I began this book I, myself, was not in the know about VOIP, although it was already out there and lots of people were loving it and swearing by it.

Now that we have the World Wide Web (also called the internet), it seems we can plug into it and send our voices over it and it our conversations will sound even better in many cases than the old fashioned telephone service in our houses where we plug those tiny little plastic plugs into the wall.

I signed up for Skype before leaving on my latest excursion to Central America in 2011. I got my very own telephone number that is exactly like any number in the San Fernando Valley, California. Getting the number cost me $30 for a whole year at a discount, because at the same time I also signed up for a monthly service fee of $7.00. This monthly fee enables me to call anywhere in the United States and talk as long as I want for nothing more than the $7.00 monthly fee. For a few more dollars I could have signed up for all the calls I could make all over the entire world!

All I need is an internet connection that works relatively well and I can talk for as long as I want to my friends and family back in the USA.

Imagine this. You call me at an 818 number as if I were in Burbank. When I am not "online" – like walking in the streets, at a restaurant or sitting on a beach, I can set up Skype to forward calls to whatever third world cell phone I happen to have and get the call as if I'd been sitting by my computer awaiting a Skype call. The person calling me only paid to call Burbank. Yet you reached me in Guatemala or wherever wherever I am with a local cell phone handy. It will cost me maybe 8 cents a minute for the call to get from my Skype number to my Guatemalan number. The caller has no idea that technology is doing such amazing things.

With such unbelievable forms of communications, that simply were not available years ago, how can we justify staying home if we have the slightest inclination to see the world?

LAPTOPS AND NOTBOOKS. When I traveled to Guatemala the first part of 2008, I did not take any technology with me as I had the idea it would be too much of a burden carrying it around and worrying about it. Since that trip amazing new technology exists in the form iPads, "notebooks," mini PCs, etc. Probably other fancy names I haven't heard of. For my latest trip I purchased a "mini" whatever you want to call it.

Used to be you would plug in such a device to charge it up and have maybe as many as 4 hours of battery power (and that was a lot) to run it once it was unplugged. My new device (that I call Baby) gives me around 9 hours of use, during which I don't need to plug into anything. Baby only weighs about 3 pounds (less than half the weight of a traditional laptop) so it's hardly even noticeable hanging around in my small every day backpack.

Before leaving on a fun trip to faraway lands, I can load onto Baby lots of movies, TV Shows and music from CDs. I have earphones that also have a microphone so they double as my Skype phone. If people are around I can

167

listen to music through the earphones while I write a book anywhere I happen to be. Or, I can watch a movie in a restaurant, even right on the beach if I have a mind to. Or watch a movie of MY choice in an airplane. "Look Ma. No cords." If there are no people around or I want to share a movie or music with others, I have dandy battery operated speakers from Radio Shack that turn Baby into a little entertainment center.

Back in the USA, as I'm sure is true with many of us, I enjoyed watching a bit of TV before slipping away to dreamland. Now, each night while away from home, I just set up Baby with some external speakers and enjoy another episode of Boston Legal or maybe a rerun of Julie and Julia that I downloaded in a restaurant at the beach in Costa Rica from iTunes. Cords not required as I have so many hours of battery backup on Baby I can just take her to bed with me.

During a trip in 2010 to Costa Rica, I resolved to complete this book and forced myself into isolation by renting a bungalow where there were NO people around to keep me from focusing. The minute I arrived it was so quiet and isolated I thought I must have made a terrible mistake and I wanted to run off immediately to more populated environs. But in the interest of productivity I resolved to stick it out for nine whole days. As soon as I set up Baby and some old familiar Norah Jones and a little Mozart I felt perfectly comfortable and no longer isolated.

Just since my trip in early 2008 up to this particular writing in 2012, an amazing thing has happened just about anywhere you go. Not only does Starbucks in the USA provide you with wireless internet, now even bars in Costa Rica and Guatemala that have nothing on their floors but sand provide wireless internet (wi-fi) for their customers. I'm betting there are similar establishments all over the world that are also now providing this high tech perk for their customers.

I'm thinking in no time at all, given how fast the technology movement is racing along, that any hotel anywhere in the world that doesn't provide wi-fi will be as frowned upon as if they had no rest rooms for their customers.

Doesn't it sound like I've spent a fortune on all that technology? NOT! I searched the World Wide Web to find the best price for Baby (it was not on ebay) and was able to adopt her for only $330 out the door. No tax (the seller was in New York State) or shipping (just 'cause that's how they do it). These days, although Baby was relatively cheap, there are even lighter weight, faster and better products with longer battery life and better everything for even less money. Just get a grandchild on the job of helping you shop for the latest thing.

When I recall the difficulties of shoestring travel before all this wonderful technology became available, I can understand why people might hesitate to take off to foreign lands. It has truly become so simplified to find out everything you could ever want to know, check on reservations, look for maps and maybe best of all we now can enjoy such close communications with our people that it's just as good as being home in our own living rooms, only better. And not to mention abundant entertainment anywhere, any time.

What if the only thing standing between you and getting on the road is a good education in technology?

Once again, even if you don't ever leave the country, learning about today's technology will NEVER be something you will regret.

EIGHT

Healthcare

I just love weird movies. During my first trip to Guatemala I saw the movie Sicko. I thought I wanted to watch it for fun but it turned out very relevant to this message. If you think you may choose to take the gypsy path but are still concerned about health care, I strongly recommend you sit down with a cold drink and a bowl of popcorn and check out this amazing Michael Moore movie. Even if you don't like Michael Moore, watch it anyway just so you can say you did. Afterwards you can always talk about how he made it all up. I personally don't believe that. But if you don't even watch it how can you know what you might think? And it might shed new light on our standard ways of thinking about health care – ala USofA.

We are easily brain washed into believing we simply cannot survive outside the United States of America because all other countries are far too primitive to provide health care comparable to the highly advanced care we are certain to receive in the USA, the most civilized nation on earth, right? Do you really buy that?

You may be surprised to discover that it is just not true.

Many concerned seniors have asked me, "But what if you get sick and need a doctor or a hospital?"

First of all, if that were to happen (it might not if you keep that positive attitude going) you would be very surprised to learn that excellent health care, frequently better than what you will find in the USofA is available all over the world. And in many countries there's a good possibility you may pay nothing at all for the care you receive.

Faith in humanity, something we don't think that much about in the USofA, is another major factor. In many foreign lands where people are driven by their hearts more than by greed, you will be amazed to discover how quickly kind souls will come to your aid if you are ill or injured.

One nervous day in an overloaded ferry on a remote lake in Guatemala I heard an interesting story from a young woman from Monterrey, California. She shared with me that she had gotten a little tipsy one night, jumped over a wall and her foot landed in a hole. She found herself limping and alone in a remote Guatemalan village. As we know, the young consider themselves to be invincible so they are, in fact, more likely to sustain injuries than us more cautious seniors. But their need for healing services is every bit as crucial, often more so. But it doesn't seem to stop them from their wanderlust, does it? Why I wonder?

This young woman, traveling extensively by herself through Central America, told me that "a woman" she encountered in some small Guatemalan village took her to a friend to heal her foot which appeared to have dislocated bones. The healer placed a stone wrapped in red cloth on the girls wrecked foot. This rock was apparently, from the looks of the treatment process, the equivalent of our MRI. During the diagnosis process with the rock, another woman pinned the young traveler to the bed and began enthusiastically praying. Having diagnosed this young lady apparently by using the rock, the healer began pushing and pulling on toes and bones. In the end the young lady walked away, good as new.

What was that all about? Was it witchcraft or could it be that modern medicine did not invent the idea that people should be healed, nor was modern medicine a trail blazer in healing techniques. Or, we might just want to believe that the girl in the ferry made the whole thing up. I am very inclined to doubt that, however. Was she just sitting there waiting for someone like me to come sit with her in a ferry and start talking about medical treatments in third world countries so she could share her pre-fabricated lies? Why on earth would she do that?

As our overloaded ferry laboriously carried us to our destinations, while listing very badly to the starboard, this young woman and I had a good laugh speculating on the grandiosity of the bill she would have received from her local ER had she experienced the same misfortune in Monterrey, California.

The need to heal is not the creation of the AMA. Nor is the need to remain healthy a concept only the FDA could possibly comprehend.

Humans have searched for and found endless effective healing practices since the beginning of time. It is unrealistic to presume that only in America is it possible to receive competent health care.

In order to feel safe in the world, while outside the borders of the USA, one must detach from the illusions that we have been so carefully conditioned to believe. Among those illusions is the misinformation that we cannot entrust our precious health to healers that are not practicing in our own country in white jackets with degrees from American schools on their walls. This "illusion," so commonly accepted by most of my fellow Americans, is simply and completely unfounded.

Concern about health care is perhaps the major concern of seniors to determine whether they choose to see the world or they choose to stay home for the duration of their golden years.

The concern is understandable, of course. However, if you dream of adventure, it will likely prove itself to be your major show stopper. Don't let it stop you in your tracks because it is, truly, only an illusion. Like pulling a rabbit out of a hat.

It may or may not be true that we pass this way but once. Just in case it's true, don't let the window of opportunity slam shut on your dreams because of nasty and very often erroneous rumors.

For every horror story your friends and acquaintances gleefully share with you about foreign health care nightmares, you, yourself, already know an equal number of health care nightmares experienced by people (perhaps your own friends and/or family) right here in the US of A.

The real truth about your health is that it is totally in your own hands – and not in the hands of your doctor at all. And, hard as it may be to accept, our health – good or bad – is largely (maybe entirely) manifested out of our minds and our attitudes.

Whether or not we travel, it is imperative we accept that reality – that our health is in OUR own hands.

If you already lean in the direction of owning your own well-being, I can recommend a good manufacturer of luggage for the serious traveler because what for most people would be the greatest obstacle to travel will, for you, have no negative impact whatsoever. You are good to go any time now.

If you can own your health and not leave it in the hands of doctors you can start now to choose interesting destinations to visit because the world will be your oyster!

The purpose of this chapter is mainly to make the reader aware that there is competent healthcare outside of the USA and it is important to not buy into the illusions that are presented to us but to use one's own creativity and explore further before giving up the entire idea of travel because of our unfounded fears about healthcare.

Before leaving the subject of healthcare, here is just a small example of a dental experiment.

A couple of weeks before leaving on a trip to Costa Rica, I broke the side off one of my teeth. Instead of going to a dentist in the USA I decided to take this real life experience to Costa Rica instead as I was headed there anyway.

Life is definitely different and I believe rather magical when one is "on the road." On Sunday Ileana, the fabulous female proprietor of Arilapa Bed and Breakfast where I was staying, happened to be escorting Lorna, another hotel guest and grandmother of a brand new baby to see a friend of Ileana's, who happens to be a baby nurse. Ileana, extremely bright and always quick to make everything work, remembered both that the nurse's daughter is a dentist and that I was in need of a dentist.

On her return to Arilapa, Ileana informed me that she had made an appointment for me the following day at 1:00 p.m. My appointment was just a few minutes bus ride down the road where I was to see her friend's daughter, "the dentist." The rest of the story is just plain amazing.

On Monday, as scheduled, I hopped onto the local bus for 25 cents and rode only for a few short moments before getting off almost at the doorstep to the dentist's office. Dr. Molina buzzed me through the locked gate and greeted me herself. You can imagine my shock to discover that this "girl child" was

175

to be my dentist. Dr. Molina looked to be about 15 years old and maybe not even quite old enough to go on a date without a chaperone. Or so it would seem to merely behold her youthful countenance.

Since fortunately I have no prejudice about young people, I was perfectly happy to put my complete faith, confidence and teeth into Dr. Molina's competent hands.

Our communication was a bit challenging as I just barely limp along with my less than fluent Spanish. Dr. Molina was in just about the same boat with English but she was very good natured and willing to struggle through our mutual communications handicaps.

Try to imagine yourself in the office of a dentist in the United States or even Canada. Can you imagine such a scenario as the following? I cannot. Here's how the business of the broken tooth went.

What broke on my tooth was not the side of a natural tooth, as I had thought and feared. It seems the particular tooth at issue is covered by a porcelain crown. Do you know exactly which of your teeth is a crown and which is not? I've certainly lost track over the years.

Dr. Molina simply explained to me but did not sell me on the "right" way to solve the problem. She told me the right solution was to completely remove the entire, existing, broken crown and replace it with a new crown. This procedure would take about three more visits and cost – are you sitting down – 100,000 colones – Costa Rica's version of money. Sounds like a fortune but translates into only about $180.00 US, based on the exchange rate on that particular day. Such an insanely low price would be completely unheard of in my country! To completely remove and replace a crown! I'm still in shock. I am well aware that in my country, even if I had dental insurance, which I don't, my share would have been more than twice that and as I would have to pay the entire amount I'm guessing over $1000 out of my meager retiree funds.

We discussed the fact that, while I could manage three appointments and the cost was certainly reasonable and affordable for the "right" solution, signing up for a three visit procedure would make my travels in Costa Rica much more complicated as I had planned to travel around for my entire stay in that beautiful country.

I asked Dr. Molina what the "wrong" or the "other" solution would be and she explained that she could simply polish the broken part of the porcelain and I could carry on with the rest of my life. Thinking this sounded too good to be true, I interrogated her as much as I possibly could, considering our language challenge, about the potential problems for this "other" and totally simplified procedure. For example, what if I chomped down again on popcorn kernels (the original culprit) and broke more of the porcelain. Could I do enough damage to expose the root and experience pain? I wanted to be sure to ward off pain if I should be on some remote little beach on a remote little island, maybe hours by uncomfortable bus and maybe even a ferry away from a dentist. The prospect of an exposed nerve while stranded did not appeal to me one bit. THAT, I thought, would be a nightmare that I should attempt to avoid if at all possible.

Dr. Molina explained to me that the metal, which is under the porcelain covering of the crown, is extremely strong and it would be pretty much impossible to do anything to that particular tooth that would result in exposing the root.

Guess which option I chose? Of course. Let's polish the remnant of the crown and I'll go on my merry way, heading for the beach as soon as possible. Decision made, the adorable young dentist cheerfully ground and polished a bit on the side of my tooth and in a few minutes my worries were over – probably for the rest of my life as far as that particular tooth is concerned and according to the girl child dentist.

Oh, I almost forgot. Your burning question. How much to solve the tooth challenge. Well, I will tell you what it finally cost me, but you will not believe me, as I can hardly believe it myself. The whopping expense for the entire thing was 5,000 colones or about $8.80 US. And, I suppose we could add in the 25 cents in transportation expense for the five minute bus ride.

Am I happy I decided to bring my dental challenge to Costa Rica? You bet I am. The money I saved actually more than paid for my entire trip to Costa Rica, including airfare and hotels.

I'm not even sure myself which part of this entire situation is most amazing to me. I find all the little pieces amazing and wonderful. Like Ileana from my hotel just taking it upon herself to get me set up with the appointment so I wouldn't have to travel so far. Then there is the incredible difference in price between the cost in Costa Rica and what the cost would have been in the USA for a complete replacement of a crown. What amazes me most of all is that the adorable young dentist cheerfully let me out of her office without my having signed up for the "right" solution. Maybe my Polyanna attitude doesn't exist when it comes to dentists. But it is inconceivable to me that any dentist in the USofA would let the opportunity to capitalize on a broken crown slip through their nimble fingers. Maybe one in 500. But I've never been fortunate to have met that one.

After this incident I wandered off to spend a month with my feet in the sand on Playa Samara, a most beautiful Costa Rican beach. When I returned to Ileana, the wonderful proprietor of Arilapa where I had been staying during the dental episode, there were two people staying there who had come to Costa Rica JUST to get their dental work done. One was a gorgeous senior citizen who had the most beautiful teeth I'd ever seen on a man. In the USA he had been quoted $46,000 for 26 implants. Just about an entire mouthful of teeth, right? He spent some weeks in Costa Rica (I don't recall how many) and got the whole job done for about $16,000.

Another guest had also come for major dental work and had saved 50% for all the work she had done, compared to what she had been quoted in the USA. Many thousands of dollars involved in her situation as well.

NINE

Homelessnes

This chapter is about buying a ticket to somewhere on a limited income. Social Security for example. But it's mostly about letting go.

Many people looking at this book may, at first glance, decide that the whole idea of seeing the world on a limited, fixed income is impossible.

Well, alright. If you say so. But I say that little in life is impossible if we use our brains, logic, a bit of faith in ourselves and if we are truly committed to our dreams.

The first question to ask yourself is if you have the courage to become intentionally homeless for a period of time. Probably not forever but long enough to explore distant lands while the possibility of doing so still exists for you.

Keep in mind the title and spirit of this book, *GET PACKING: If Not Now, When?*

Money aside, there is something you may have at 65 that you may not have at 75. That something may be the last vestiges of your good health and strength, not to mention the good fortune of still having your wits about you.

I don't mean to be an alarmist but let's be realistic. We are not getting any younger and we are going to die before too awfully much longer. To put it bluntly and tell you what you already know but may not want to look at, nobody is getting out of this alive.

So look at what you value most. How you will live, or how you will die.

Recently I was reading some great spiritual wisdom from Buddhists or Taoists – I forget which but does it really matter? The guidance was all about attachments or rather detachment. It specifically suggested that the trick is to die before you die.

I took this to mean that we should let go while we still are living because when we die we no longer have the luxury of choice. How silly to repeat what we already know so well. But I will do it anyway. The simple truth about everything in our lives is that we can't take it with us. What is this? New information? Gotta doubt it!!!

When we die we no longer will think about whether or not we can give up our cars, kids, tools, granny's crystal, 36 purses, 48 pairs of shoes, etc., etc. All bets are off and all that stuff stays behind whether we agree to that or not.

All those "things" - that stuff that defined us for a lifetime - can become someone else's anchor now, or later – or perhaps or maybe more likely, it can become someone else's trash. Right now the choice is yours. Later it will not be.

Detaching now will even provide you the added benefit of experiencing the enjoyment of the recipients of your "stuff."

What am I saying? What am I not so subtly hinting at? Is it the unthinkable for you? To part with your stuff?

Let me say it straight out so you can get over the shock before we move on to the fun parts.

Get rid of your stuff!

If that sounds too radical an idea, even if the payoff is adventure and freedom, then accept reality. The reality is that *you* do not own your stuff anyway. If you can't part with it, then your stuff owns you. Do you really want to go to your grave at the mercy of your possessions?

NOTE: Remember if you are well heeled in old age, this is not the book for you. These wild ideas are meant for those of us who must, from necessity, live on limited income because that's how it's turned out for us and now we are going to make the very best of it. If that is NOT you and you choose to read this anyway, you already realize that you can have the luxury of keeping all your stuff and still take off to wherever you choose. So what's holding you back? Go pack. You can travel in safer and more comfortable ways than us retirees living on very limited, fixed incomes. Via con Dios.

If money is not an issue for you, yet you haven't taken off by the time you are 66 years old, you either have no desire to travel or some of the fears and considerations covered in this book may be obstacles to your departure.

For those whose freedom will be difficult or impossible while maintaining a home base, here are some suggestions for handling the material anchors that hold you to earth.

This process can take some time so the sooner you start thinking about this the better because, after all, if not now when?

When people look around at all they own, they usually see the collection of their worldly possessions as a whole. "My stuff." Unfortunately, some people find themselves so attached to their possessions that they have difficulty distinguishing themselves as actually separate from their stuff.

Of course, now that we know about cells and atoms we are all well aware that nothing on earth is that simple.

This is a wonderful time to dissect, evaluate and disseminate the entire anchor that you have up to now thought of as all your worldly goods.

In reality all you will be doing is what your family or someone will have to do anyway when you leave this life. You are simply seizing the opportunity to have your own control over the material aspects of your life that you have declared to be so meaningful.

*NOTE: About dying. I know I bring it up fairly frequently and I certainly don't mean to be negative or depressing – only realistic. The golden years are a very special time of life. Like childhood, falling in love, getting married, parenthood, the whole huge chunk of our professional lives, etc. Retirement, this very special time of life, which I like to call THE BIG THANK YOU, can be many amazing things and should be our reward for all our hard work. But we must remember that time is of the essence and in the end we will not move on to the next - another phase of **this** life. We may or may not move on to another lifetime. But that remains to be seen and it's difficult to make solid plans for that particular future.*

So, once again, I must reiterate – no one is getting out of this alive. Failing to get a good, solid, realistic grasp on that certainly could cause a person to fail to act in the direction of his or her dreams.

The window of opportunity WILL close. Don't let it slam shut on you before you get a chance to jump right through it, like Alice stepping through the looking glass.

You are more than your stuff. You are your dreams.

Now back to living your dreams.

Any of this sound like anything you have said to yourself? Thoughts you have been holding on to:

Don't be silly. I can't afford to travel on Social Security.
I have too much "stuff" to worry about.
How can I leave my family?
I have to pay rent.
I have to keep paying the mortgage.
What about my dog? Cat? Bird? Plants?
I could never part with my portrait of my Topsy kitty.
What about my favorite pillow?
What would I do with my grandmother's dishes?
But I've got 30 purses and 40 pairs of shoes.
What about my 14 boxes of Christmas decorations?
How about health care? I'm, not getting any younger.
How about my tools? Gotta have 'em.
My cars?
My friends?
The crystal I got 40 years ago at my 1st wedding?

In dealing with the "anchor" of your stuff it will be necessary to dissect the whole, breaking it into logical and disposable parts.

Begin with the obvious, the easiest chore so you can get into the spirit of liberation without too much stress. Practice, practice, practice. And in no time you will be free to walk lightly about the planet.

Think thrift store. You've done this many times before and it's pretty painless, usually. Fun in fact. You can easily approach your first layer of disposable junk and the prospect of sharing with the needy as even an activity that will leave you with a pretty good feeling. So forget that this may get more challenging and just do a routine spring cleaning of all those things you've been saying you need to get cart off to the thrift store. You were already planning to do this, weren't you?

Try to push just a tad beyond what you might normally have eliminated. Many people who are very successful at NOT accumulating too much junk suggest you use a kind of timeline. For example, if you go through your closet and discover things you haven't worn in say 12 months (or whatever period of time you choose) designate them for the thrift store. That can surely be a challenge because most people will find things they have never worn even once – often with tags still attached. But be strong. Be disciplined. It will only hurt for a little while and then you will forget all about those things. In time you'll forget how much you paid for them a year ago when you just couldn't live without them.

As a side note, this might be a good time to remember how badly you thought you needed "stuff" that was just abandoned once you put it into your closet. That exercise may help you to get more and more clear about how strongly we can attach to material possessions when in truth they mean very little (or nothing at all) to us. It is not the "thing" we wanted so badly but the acquisition of the thing. The "rush" of the purchase. The feeling of buying.

So for this first, easy step, press on just past your comfort zone – just for practice.

Gather all your bags and boxes together and ponder them for a while. Think about how this happened. How long did it take to collect that stuff? What kept you from parting with it before this? What will it be like to enjoy the space you will have after the removal of all that junk!

I must caution you about a peculiar phenomenon you may experience when you begin to consciously dispose of your "anchors" piece by piece. You may become addicted to dissemination of your possessions. It may become a rush – obverse to the one you felt on acquisition of the items. But none the less a rush.

Addictions come from wanting to revisit a desired feeling. As you begin to experience the feeling of freedom from unburdening yourself of your belongings, you may become increasingly enthusiastic about discovering just one more white elephant you can live without.

If you have the room or can make the room, it's great fun and far easier to begin to designate sections of your home for items headed to various destination. I set up my bedroom at my most active moment of relieving myself of stuff as a kind of triage area and then had great fun saying, "And this is the Goodwill corner. Here are the books for the library. These things go to the grandkids." Etc. I actually moved my bed into the living room just to afford myself one whole room to use to sort everything that was going – in one direction or another.

Your challenge may be vastly simplified if you have family to whom you would logically will your belongings as part of your final legacy. On the other hand, imagine how enlightening it might be to discover so early in the game that those family members don't really want that beautiful painting of your dog Topsy, who you treasured but who, sadly, passed away in 1960, before your children were even born. What a wonderful opportunity to spare them the confusion of trying to decide what to do with items that were treasures to you but mean absolutely nothing to them. You can be sure that if they are not anxious to hang Topsy in the den now, they would be equally disenchanted at that prospect once you have departed this life.

In which case, consider the service you are providing them by relieving them of having to experience the guilt of tossing Topsy later.

If you love your children, which of course you do, why not simply their futures by simplifying yours NOW?

It may be useful to insert a step between the thrift store and family treasures. Again just for practice. For this kind of middle step you will want to give serious thought to how out on a limb you are willing to or want to take yourself in your travel adventures. You may want to actually hold onto some items in storage for a time in case you want to set up housekeeping again. If you do this, try very hard NOT to attach a monthly price tag to storing your stuff. Find a friend or family member with a free corner in a garage for your stuff to rest in peace for a while.

I made the choice to plow full speed ahead into unlimited adventures for as long as I can think straight and climb stairs. My theory was that should I again want to settle in the USA, in my own space, I could probably acquire all the household items I would need for a few hundred dollars at a thrift store. My option was to hold onto enough household items to furnish a small apartment. But the cost over time might be more than replacing them. Also, those items would continue to be an ongoing part of my anchor. Decisions, decisions.

So for the interesting second layer of your onion, look at two aspects.

Consider things you have that you don't need and may never actually need. (Truthfully, all you really need is a passport, suitcase, a toothbrush and a few clothes anyway.) But this stuff we're talking about is good and you really like it or liked it and you just can't bring yourself to just give it away to strangers.

With any luck and if you have some really fine "stuff" you can always set up garage or apartment sales and get some money in exchange for your treasures. Part of the shock of the garage sale route is discovering how little other people think your "valuables" are worth. There could be two ways to look at that phenomenon.

One might be to feel really bad that the world sees so little value in what you hold dear. The other might be to accept enlightenment (a hard pill to swallow) that stuff you thought was so valuable isn't really that big a deal after all – to anybody but you.

One way of looking at it won't get you moving but only make you sad. The other could contribute to your letting go just a little bit more so you can finally fly off into your dreams.

The shedding of the clutter of your life might be a multi-stage project. You might get yourself all the way to homeless, take a trip or two and return home to look again at what you thought was so darned important. You might then part with another large pile of "stuff" and wander off on another adventure to who knows where. This exercise of liberation might even to be run through a few times.

But what liberation is available for you if you can truly lighten your load in this lifetime! Imagine finally taking off knowing that you can be gone as long as you want and wander off wherever you want because you have pulled up anchor once and for all.

If you rent a house or apartment your task is, of course, very simple. Just give notice and away you go. If you own a home you are one lucky vagabond. You can rent your home and create income to help you travel around. Or you could do a reverse mortgage on your home and create income to help you travel around. I realize many people think a reverse mortgage is terrible. Bad business and how can we do that to the kids?!?!?! Well what ever happened to it's your turn? Of course, if you simply could NEVER bring yourself to deny your family the yield of all YOUR many years of YOUR hard work, then I guess you could always just stay home and watch TV and wait for the kids to inherit. There are pretty good travel shows these days. That option, however, is just not what this book is about.

Once you get rid of the "stuff" of your life that you must provide a dwelling to house, and once you have figured out how to vacate your dwelling, there isn't too much more to do but GET PACKING. Since we've already covered how little you need to take and how much you need to NOT take, might as well get the travel plan underway.

That is after you have fully convinced yourself that it is really OK for you to leave the rest behind. That is the people you love.

TEN

The Worst Thing That Can Happen

When one door of happiness closes, another opens;
but often we look so long at the closed door
that we do not see the one which has been opened for us.

- Helen Keller
-

This book is about the precious gift of life. It is not just about living it to the fullest. It is about not wasting the gift of life and it is about getting on with your dreams NOW.

It seems too painfully ironic that during the initial writing of this book my beloved son Joey and my dear high school chum Carol Ann (always Sweet Caroline to me) both passed away. Then, less than a month after my son Joey passed away on February 10th, my dear friend Jon died, completely unexpectedly in his sleep.

Sweet Caroline was taken by cancer almost at the exact time she reached the age of Uncle Sam's criteria for full retirement. Sweet Caroline never made it to THE BIG THANK YOU.

My son's life ended when he was only 41 years old, after 15 to 20 years of struggle with mental illness and addiction.

Pat, Jon's wonderful wife had just completed handling for me all the mortuary arrangements for my son Joe. I learned of Jon's death on calling Pat to tell her I had just finished paying for Joe's cremation. On that very call she answered her phone to tell me Jon had just died in his sleep. How could such a thing as still another death even happen? Jon worked for the State of California in what he seemed to feel was a very dull and pointless position. Jon spoke so very often about his plans for retirement but Jon also never made it to THE BIG THANK YOU.

On the terrible night I learned of Joey's death I was living in Guatemala where I was interviewing senior citizens who had already taken on the path to adventure that I propose in this book.

As a mother, my first instinct on hearing of Joey's death was, of course, to catch the next flight back to California. But I soon enough realized, and my friends pressed me into understanding, that Joey was gone. There was no longer anything I could do for him. My years of trying to save him had yielded only pain and frustration and, of course, had not cured his mental illness.

Through the worst tragedy a mother can encounter I came to understand that clearly the intention of this book is to promote "LIFE" - which had become a passionate message for me – especially when looking so closely at the agony of losing someone I loved so much. I wanted to promote the full expression of the precious gift of LIFE. In particular my intention in producing this book was to lure mothers and fathers who gave their all to their families and work duties for 50 years to seize the rest of their lives and find ways to color them joy and fun.

It is your turn after all.

The morning after I learned of my son's death I was sitting in a restaurant crying my eyes out, drinking coffee and watching a parade of Guatemalans pass me on their way to their jobs and endless children all spiffed up for school. I was in the process of an agonizing internal battle over whether to stay and continue with the writing of this book or return to the U.S.A. I realized that I my return to California was mostly inspired by the belief that

I "should" return in spite of the reality that there was nothing that required my personal attention because an army of helpers were at the ready to do whatever they could to support me in this tragedy. Good friends were there who lovingly urged me to stay and continue with this project.

In the village where I was staying at the time, most all the women still wear the clothes of their Mayan culture. The indigenous Mayan people are graceful, lovely, friendly and amazingly free with their smiles. But after spending many weeks in villages around Lake Atitlan I had come to understand how incredibly challenged these people are in so many ways.

The country has been plagued by foreign bullies and wars that had nothing whatsoever to do with these beautiful people but impacted them in the most tragic possible ways. Despite their tragic history, their smiles never seem to fade. They have lost their own sons and daughters to stupid wars, terrible traffic, bad water, hurricanes, floods and illness. And what place on earth is free of the tragic miseries and deadly results of mental illness and addictions? Not even in the beautiful highlands of Guatemala.

An entire village that I could have seen just across the lake, if it were still there, was completely washed away during Hurricane Stan in 2005. Hundreds of souls perished. But the smiles of these amazing people never fade.

They teach me, simply by being who they are, all about the human potential to survive and thrive and continue smiling.

As I watched the smiling Guatemalans wandering by that morning, I knew that every one of them had suffered tragedies at the very least equal to what I was dealing with. I made my decision to stay in Guatemala and continue working on my book about LIFE. I would not run away into my illusion that absolutely nothing could possibily be handled relative to my son's death, without my omnipotent intervention. Were I omnipotent I might, indeed, have saved his life.

In the course of preparing for and embarking on my journey to Guatemala I had discovered that I did somehow live with the illusion of omnipotence with regard to motherhood. At some point I came face to face with the realization that I am not God. Just a loving and very dedicated mother.

Perhaps as parents we do have a tendency to fancy ourselves as having God-like qualities. And perhaps this illusion makes our job of letting go of our children all the more impossible for so many of us.

Many will say that leaving the country, as I am proposing; is simply out of the question because their children need them. If you are around the commonly accepted retirement age of 65, your children are at least 30 years old and more likely closer to and even past 40. When will he/she/they be old enough to be on their own?

No mother on earth was ever more into the quicksand illusions of God-like motherhood beliefs than I. No mother ever spent more time and money on psychologists, books and journals than I did. Until I finally had read and learned enough to come to my senses. I am NOT God.

Now my beloved son is gone. Shall I take to my own grave a God-like illusion that I failed him in some way? That had I not left the United States he would still be alive?

You and I both know that a belief that I had the power to keep my son alive would be irrational. Holding onto the belief that our adult children will not survive without us is simply not rational and is, in fact, an insult to our children.

So let us accept that the very worst that could ever happen might actually happen. We could lose a child while out of the country. It happened to me. And let us also accept that as parents, in almost every single instance, we do not have the power to save our adult children whether they be on the next street, the next city or in the next continent.

If you are a parent of an adult child or children and having trouble packing your stuff after reading this entire book, come back to this chapter. Read it again and wonder if you are able to detach from any God-like parental habits.

Parenthood is meant to be a joy and, for a certain number of years, maybe a joy AND a duty. But, although we will certainly experience lifelong love, it is not meant to be a lifelong career.

Once again, it is your turn.

ELEVEN

Saving Up – Breaking Free – Taking Off

This entire process is going to take some planning and patience but hurry! The patience we should have learned in the process of evolving into senior citizens and your newly evolved patience as a bona fide senior citizen will be extremely helpful as you launch into a new, full life of fun and adventure. But hurry!

There may be parts of the process of preparing for the next step that will not be necessary for many of you so you can just skip those.

This book's focus is for seniors on limited incomes and in keeping with that focus we shall leave no stone unturned.

However, I realize you likely will be gleaning from this book only what applies to you. You may have a home you can rent out easily and profitably or if you own it you can consider a reverse mortgage to fund your travel. Perhaps you even have sufficient money in the bank to buy all the tickets you want without any challenge whatsoever. In that case, what are you waiting for? Certainly skip this section and maybe even the entire book and GET PACKING!

However, some of these ideas may sound like fun for you whether you ever leave the country or not and whether you have no need to save any money at all.

Some of these ideas absolutely stand on their own as wonderful experiences and a great use of your time, whatever your financial situation.

For those who want or need an opportunity to save money for tickets and get used to the idea of being "home free," (or you might say homeless) this section is designed to create a launching site for a new and freer beginning.

This is the decompression part of the worldwide adventure process. This next little part is to offer you a safe harbor in the USosA before the real foreign adventure gets underway.

During this early stage you discover the joy of being "homefree" while exploring the mysteries of life and death in a safe environment within the USA.

In this first little possibility you are provided a safe, comfortable place to sleep, three fabulous and healthy meals a day, classes in spirituality and other fascinating subjects, an opportunity for as much exercise as you want, even, perhaps, including yoga lessons. You will live in a setting of natural beauty, surrounded by amazing people, most of whom will share your interest in adventure and the exploration and discovery of the meaning of life.

Sound too good to be true? And this is the part where you save up for your airplane ticket? You know what they say, that when something sounds too good to be true it usually isn't true. In this, case, however, it is true. And, it's potentially even better than what I've just described.

All this potential fun will cost you anywhere from zero dollars a month to around $250 a month. Even if your social security income is only $600 a month you could still potentially save enough money in just one month to buy a ticket to somewhere. This is true because as outlined in the Chapter **"Homelessness"** you are no longer going to be paying for rent, utilities (cable, electricity, gas, internet, telephone), food and perhaps not even for the expense of an automobile - including insurance, registration, gas, oil and maintenance. Don't you feel lighter just thinking about that much freedom?

Here is the secret. It's called "work exchange". It comes in many flavors depending on what you enjoy doing and/or are willing to do.

First I must say there are other methods to save a few hundred dollars to buy an airplane ticket and airplane tickets don't even cost as much as you might think.

You could just continue working at the same old job after you start receiving your Social Security. But you can get very stuck in that like quicksand because in doing that you will need to continue to support yourself, provide shelter, buy food, etc. The concept of "If Not Now, When?" will seem rather silly if you don't even start thinking that way until you're 75. That just will not do.

The work exchange is ideal because it takes you immediately out of your drab, everyday existence and allows you to begin a whole new life of learning and adventure almost immediately.

In general the work exchange experience provides you room and meals for little or nothing in terms of financial output.

Your accommodation – sleeping situation – can range from a "bring your own tent and sleeping bag and enjoy our cold showers and outhouse" to a very cozy, even possibly modern and private room with nearby shower and toilet facilities. Private bathroom is highly unlikely.

Some people fully enjoy the most rustic accommodations. I have been in facilities where, when the tent people are told that winter has come and they must move inside, there is considerable resistance, despite the chillier or downright cold weather.

As far as I know so far, for myself, I prefer a step up from a tent. But with every day that passes I discover my appetite and willingness for new experiences expands. By this time next year I may be bored with indoor living and prefer a tent. How would I know that at this point?

For many people the concept of a common shower house (albeit with private showers and toilets) would be highly distasteful. But I must share that some of the most enjoyable times of my work exchange experience have been unplanned meetings with the girls, dishing dirt, sharing stories and telling jokes late at night in the "shower house". This kind of serendipity is just more justification for taking along a sense of humor, an open mind and a positive mental attitude. Without those personal qualities it is entirely possible – no probable in fact – that some great potential memories will be completely missed. But, of course, without those personal qualities life - no matter where you are - is not going to be all that much fun anyway.

If you like camping but also wish to be on your own and feel completely safe, then consider the possibility of tent life – out with the deer and frogs and sky's at night that will take your breath away.

If, like myself, you prefer a real bed inside a real structure, but do enjoy company as well, a room for two with a roommate you have never met before might be perfect for you.

Now and then you may encounter a roommate you just cannot stomach. But my experience has been completely positive. Keep in mind, however, that this is an adventure and not a bed of roses. Keep your positive mental attitude in action and the likelihood of getting a roommate your just can't stand will no doubt be avoided in the first place.

A happy word about roommates.

One of my roommates at a retreat that I enjoyed very much was a young lady of 17 who turned 18 just a week after she arrived at the retreat. My first thought was, "Oh my God! A teenager. What now!" This incredible young woman is from Russia. Siberia of all places. She managed with incredible strength and intention to get herself to the USA by signing up for a work exchange at a children's camp in New England. There she earned $400 and somehow managed to get to California to the particular yoga retreat where I met her. Her interest, at the tender age of only 17, was to learn yoga and meditation and return to Siberia and teach people in her town these practices.

We continue to be in touch after many years of our meeting and I know without a doubt that we will be friends for life. I expect that we will meet, I am hoping in Siberia or perhaps in California, sometime in the future.

Just goes to show. You meet the nicest people in work exchange programs.

Another of my roommates was a tiny young woman of about 28 who works, weather permitting, for the forest service. She works exclusively in wilderness areas where vehicles and any kind of fuel driven or noisy equipment are absolutely not permitted. She and her co-workers must carry in all supplies and carry out all their trash. Her job, before winter comes, among other things, includes moving trees that have fallen across paths. The crew is only able to use hand tools including 100 year old hand saws and human leverage.

This young forest ranger spends winters in the somewhat warmer areas of the California Sierra Nevada Mountains in a work exchange program where she focuses on yoga, meditation and her spiritual practices until the snow melts and she can return to her normal everyday duties as the tiniest lumber jack in history.

Which only goes to show. You meet the nicest people in work exchange programs.

Should you be totally OK with lots of company, the world truly is your oyster and you can see places, meet people and have experiences you never dreamed possible.

In that case, with regard to sleeping and the necessities of life, there are some excellent exchange programs providing bunks in dorms.

One truly beautiful spiritual retreat that I know of asks a very minor fee of $50 per month and perhaps an equal amount for a non-refundable registration fee. Their accommodation when last I heard was in a 24 bunk dorm room.

While some of you may cringe at the thought of all those people living in the same room, the more adventurous may recognize the amazing opportunity in this type of environment to meet and often establish lifelong relationships with some of the most amazing, out of the box people on earth.

It is also a great opportunity to toughen up your spirit and discover that you can, in fact, do things you never dreamed you could or would do.

Finally, you may come across an arrangement where you have your own very private room. It happens, believe it or not. If that would be your preference, know that this would just be your good fortune. Perhaps an offshoot of that positive mental attitude you have polished up just for this adventure.

A private room does not tend to be the norm but some facilities just happen to have private rooms or on occasion you may by staying in a room for two and, for one reason or other, you simply do not happen to have a roommate during all or part of your stay.

How long can you handle this type of lifestyle? Some programs have minimum commitments of two to four months. Some have a maximum period of stay from two to four months.

From the facility's perspective, training a person, incorporating that person into the routine and then having that person leave too soon would not be a good business practice. So it makes sense for them to have at least a two month commitment. Of course, if you find you absolutely can't handle the whole thing, you cannot be burned at the stake and there is often a two week probationary period as with most jobs these days.

Maximum length of stay also makes perfect sense from a business perspective. Many people fall in love with the work exchange life-style and never want to leave. Once you do it you will understand.

There are some places where it may be possible to stay on in a different capacity. In some cases you might be a paid participant instead of a paying participant. Don't expect if you make any money at all that it be much. The purpose of this book is to guide you into a new life of adventure. Not to find you a new job.

In the spirit of launching your new life as a person who is home free and in search of adventure, my recommendation for length of stay in a work exchange is 3 or 4 months. This will give you an opportunity to save up for a ticket to somewhere exotic. It will also give you a safe environment to experience the freedom of being home free without having to leave the good old U.S.A. And you won't even need to get a passport yet.

There are a number of possible types of work exchange programs and I'm sure some I have never heard about that you may encounter in your own search.

Those I know about and find inviting for my own personal tastes are spiritual retreats and organic farms.

Spiritual retreats, while offering enlightenment are, in fact, businesses. They generally provide classes or other spiritual experiences of some type for their volunteers since their volunteers are either paying THEM or working absolutely for free. But nothing happens in life without some exchange of money. Spiritual retreats are not philanthropic entities that exist for the exclusive purpose of doing good deeds. That certainly does not mean they are a bunch of money grabbing mercenaries. Far from it. But it is important to understand from the start that business is business.

That said, you will almost always find spiritual retreats full to the brim with staffs of sincere people who are seriously motivated to follow their own spiritual paths.

It is important to understand that a work exchange program is quite different from being a paying guest at a spiritual retreat. Paying guests are pampered and an abundance of programs will be thrown at their feet. In a work exchange program you work. You might do anything from sweeping floors to making beds and doing gardening. But usually you don't work too awfully hard or long and many, many wonderful meals, classes and other educational and enlightening benefits are offered.

Because there is much to offer spiritual seekers in a facility designed to that end, it is not only a good business practice but also a wonderful opportunity for people who become involved in a work exchange arrangement.

There are as many types of retreats as there are religions and teachers. My particular interests tend to be in spiritual eastern practices. So I prefer to be in facilities where I can learn about Buddhism, Hinduism and related teachings. Of course these practices tend to include yoga practice and meditation so you will find many yoga retreats throughout the United States and, of course, throughout the entire world.

A spiritual retreat typically provides accommodation, fabulous meals (usually or often vegetarian) and other services. The facilities are generally in the business of offering training, yoga, silent retreats, yoga teacher trainings, etc. to people who pay often fairly high prices for their services over usually several days. Accommodation for guests can be as varied as that described for work exchange program participants. Everything from tent pads to very nice rooms with private bathrooms.

Many people come to spiritual retreats with their tents because they enjoy tenting or because it's more affordable. They may then join in the usually delicious meals three times a day and they may or may not participate in various courses offered. Many people come to retreats just for their own private quiet time away from it all.

The advantages for the paying guests over simply going camping are significant. The participant can set up their tent on property that is usually an extremely safe environment. A retreat offers a safe opportunity to meditate alone in a beautiful setting or with others at designated times.

Tenting participants need not bring food or all the items required for food storage and preparation.

Paying participants, can meet, share with and learn from like minded people whose accommodation may include anything from tents to elegant private room. All of that is true for the work exchange participant as well.

One of the beautiful aspects of the work exchange program in spiritual retreats is that it allows people who cannot afford to be paying the going rate to be a guest. Yet in a work exchange program one can derive most of the same benefits from practices and classes that the paying guests are enjoying.

If you believe a stay of three or four months at a spiritual retreat would be beneficial for you and if you can see how this concept could allow you to save money, I encourage you to consider the following.

Please do not consider spending time in a work exchange program at a spiritual retreat unless you have a sincere interest in the particular practices and concepts at a specific retreat.

Earlier one of the pre-requisites outlined in this book for being a successful shoestring traveler was a cursory knowledge of email and web searching. These will be your doorway to finding the perfect retreats for you. To make one more little plug for getting knowledgeable about the latest technologies, I don't honestly know how one would find a spiritual retreat WITHOUT the internet. But with it there is not end to the possibilities you can track down in no time!!!

Any facility large enough to offer work exchange will have a website that will in most cases explain their exchange program. Most will provide a means to submit an application either electronically (fill it out right on the computer screen) or by printing, filling out and sending via snail mail. Generally there will also be an outline of work offered, applicable fees, if any, minimum or maximum stay guidelines, etc.

Again, I urge you to only consider submitting an application after you have explored and find you have a sincere interest in the practices and teaching of the retreat/s you choose.

In completing your application there are two things to remember. Express your sincere interest in learning about the teachings of the retreat to which you are applying.

I would not recommend submitting an application to participate in a work exchange program at any retreat simply as a way to save money. It is important in all we do, always, to be ethical and authentic.

However, I do believe that when we have reached retirement and move closer to the grand finale of our lives we have by that point gained some greater serenity, patience and perhaps a naturally keener interest in the spiritual aspects of life. For this reason a retreat experience as one begins their journey into an expanded and more colorful future can be highly beneficial in a number of ways.

First and perhaps most important it is an opportunity to learn more about spiritual matters and, if you choose to, immerse yourself in the pursuit of enlightenment. You will already be in the perfect environment for such an endeavor.

Most retreats offer meditation and/or yoga practice.

Meditation is touted by spiritual leaders, psychologists and health professionals as being extremely healthful and valuable for everyone. Meditation is also good for dreamers and those looking for healing and direction.

When I registered at a yoga retreat to participate in their work exchange program I went with the intention to meditate regularly, diligently and discover my purpose for the rest of my life or at least for a few years. While this may seem a simplistic notion, I can only say that my intentions to find direction through meditation and spiritual guidance were completely realized and you are now holding in your hands the culmination of that direction.

Our intentions can be mighty powerful stuff and when combined with meditation there is no telling what great ideas may pop into your head. Those ideas may have nothing to do with travel at all. If not, enjoy wherever your spirit may lead you.

At the retreat where I found my path into the pages of this book, those of us who participate in the work exchange program are referred to as karma yogis. This is a common thing to call people who are in action performing self-less service.

One of my fellow karma yogis was exploring the opportunities for work exchange programs in organic farms and shared with me some information she had gathered about an organization called WWOOF or World Wide Organization of Organic Farmers. I had never heard of such a thing and was completely enthralled.

It seems there are organic farms all over the world where people can work in exchange for a place to sleep and meals.

Many organic farms also include a spiritual aspect because they tend to be run by ecologically conscious people who also will generally have a variety of spiritual interests.

When submitting an application for an organic farm your spiritual interests would probably be less significant since the purpose of the farm is more likely to be the growing and selling of organic produce than the pursuit of spiritual enlightenment.

Most organic farms will probably not have a formal application process as with larger retreats but will instead negotiate your participation via email or on the telephone.

We are all drawn to different pastimes and I have offered here only two that I found of particular interest to me. I discovered many other possibilities exist and was overjoyed that there are so many ways people can go to great places, find fascinating companions, spend their days doing fun or at least satisfying work and all without the hum drum existence of simply paying the rent, utilities and still trying to eat better than the dogs do.

Again, to discover the perfect work exchange program for yourself, it is very important that you have at least a cursory knowledge of using the World Wide Web. We should so thrilled that technology has opened up the entire world for our exploration and pleasure. So if you are resisting – and I know you resisters are out there – just stop!!!

TWELVE

The Boomer Advantage

Many senior citizens resist and resent technology. We are experts at expressing the attitude, "What is this world coming to?" And, I must admit there are days when, if I hear one more time "press 1 for English" or "that was not an option" I would be thrilled at the opportunity to break the telephone over some evil techie's head.

I encourage those of you who fit into that group of resisters of what this world is coming to, to open you minds while there is still time.

Those of us who are at the moment around the age of 65 have been handed so many incredible gifts in so many ways. If you think about all these gifts you should understand why, as the title of this book implies, I am, somewhat obnoxiously at times, pushing you rather persistently to seize the moment.

Briefly, here are some of the gifts I see that we, our generation, have been given.

Social Security. It hasn't always been there for seniors, although I think we forget about that. It doesn't exist in many places.

If you are getting it now or are just about to start getting it you are likely to receive benefits for the rest of your life, barring a major upheaval of the entire planet that totally takes our country down.

Let's be optimistic and presume that Uncle Sam will simply drop your money into your checking account each month and you can pull it out with a plastic card at an ATM just about anywhere in the world, even when the banks are closed.   And this gift is brought to you courtesy of our friend, technology.

We are beginning to accept the sad possibility that our children and grandchildren may not receive Social Security benefits but will need instead to plan very, very carefully or depend on charity and/or their children as oldies did back in the old days. Let's pray that NEVER happens.

The State of the Planet. I have a friend who loves to say, "The world has gone to hell in a hand basket!" I've never understood what that meant but many of us believe things have gotten really bad in the world. In some ways I'm sure that's true and maybe my next book will be about that but does that really seem a good project for a Pollyanna person? Gotta doubt it, however, since I see the glass as half full and I, personally believe the world to be a pretty fabulous and inviting place. There are few countries on earth that you can't explore in varying degrees of safety and comfort. That we can now do that, I consider to be a huge gift to our generation. It hasn't always been that way and it may not always be that way. But it is now. Should we pass up this opportunity?

This positive condition of the planet is truly a window of opportunity. An idea whose time has come. Especially if you look back over the entirety of the 6 plus decades since you were born. – probably you too were born into the middle of a world war or just on the brink of it or the end of it.

Don't let this window of opportunity of a relatively peaceful world close on you. If Not Now, When?

Transportation. For all our resentment and resistance to technology, how about jet planes?

When our parents and everyone's parents before us wanted to see the world and there was an ocean in the way, they certainly had a choice. One choice. Ship and that was it. Period. Now we are blessed with the possibility of being in Boston for breakfast and Berlin for dinner.

How can we resent and resist technology that offers us such miraculous opportunities. How can we not consider technology our best friend?

Health. I'm not presuming that all the members of my generation are in great health so I'm certainly not making a generalization here. But statistically, today many people around age 65 are in excellent health. This despite the fact that the FDA allows us to eat junk that will make us sick and kill us but limits with an undying passion our access to information and understanding of natural products and services that could be highly beneficial to our health.

Whereas 50 years ago a person 65 years old was probably truly past good health and productivity, today that is not the case.

We are offered a gift which I also see as a window of opportunity. The more future generations learn about maintaining health, the longer they will live. Uncle Sam will begin to pay them Social Security benefits later in life. The schedules to prove this point are already in place.

So Americans in the future may very well end up healthier and live longer lives but perhaps without Social Security.

Once again we should be grateful that we end up with the good fortune of having better health at 65 than past generations AND we receive Social Security benefits perhaps based on an outdated idea that people at 65 are no longer inclined to be productive and so should retire from the working

213

world. Those two coincidences in my mind offer an extremely unique window of opportunity that didn't exist before and may fade out of the picture later.

Social Acceptance. Unlike in U.S.A. society, in most other countries in the world senior citizens are respected and appreciated. Could it be simply for the innate wisdom gained from having lived so many years that they are held with such high esteem?

However, for some reason that escapes me, people in other countries continue to strive to emulate Americaa social customs, dress, music, entertainment, etc. Could this "trying to be like us" result in people in other countries beginning to regard their senior population as insignificant? Which is more and more how seniors are held in the USA? Could we be looking at another window of opportunity that might potentially close before long in the USA? And if other countries want to emulate the USA, perhaps similar attitudes could develop in other countries that previously respected and admired seniors.

At the moment us seniors might still be greeted in foreign lands as welcome, respected visitors.

THIRTEEN

How Long is Long Enough?

I have my own theories on the joys of travel and they may differ drastically from yours and other people's. In fact, I know they do.

My particular life is about people. I care about people and, of course I too, as most folks, am overwhelmed with the vast oceans of humanity and the hopeless feeling that there isn't much we can do to make a difference in the world.

Even when our intentions are wonderful, still we are just one speck of good intentions in a sea of heartache.

Travel, especially travel to the destinations that are affordable, will bring us face to face with the tragic realities of the lives of people who survive in very challenging conditions.

You may not care to be confronted with this reality and that is perfectly great. Before you decide to stay home forever with your TV I want to share with you that there is an enormous potential for joy in truly making friends with people in other countries who, despite their challenges, continue to love, smile and laugh. In fact, I have come to know so many people who are dirt poor, yet love, laugh and seem to be living with more joy and grace than many Americans.

Many Americans who should consider themselves comfortable with their FDA safe food, safe houses, government programs, safe roads and the constitution to protect them are still, strange as it seems, grumpy old men and grumpy old women.

There was a time in my youth when I had a passionate desire to visit India. But, at the same time I was overwhelmed with everything about it. Of all the countries I have long to visit, India was the only one to which I was too intimidated to consider visiting without a travelling companion. So I used to mention to people my desire to visit India, in case I might encounter a kindred spirit to accompany me there.

I remember some people who responded with anger toward the Indian people who live in abject poverty. It seemed they were angry with people who could be so poor and still happy, in spite of their painful existence.

When I was much younger I remember simply being baffled at such a response, wondering why the ability to be happy in the face of poverty and struggle was not considered a wonderful quality as it seemed to me it certainly is. And not something to be condemned.

As the years passed and I came to understand the seductive nature of materialism, I gained a clearer perspective on the attitude of condemnation of the poor.

Apparently our press to achieve material wealth and our love affair in the USA with amassing stacks of money brings many to believe that crawling out poverty is possible for anyone. I seriously doubt that it is possible for everyone to crawl and claw their way out of poverty simply by coveting the material aspects of life.

What about those who will never rise above their plight. Especially those in countries where there is nothing to fall back on at all – just as most of us forget was true in the mighty USA less than 100 years ago. And for many is true today.

If you read this book and take the concepts to heart perhaps you will realize your amazing opportunity to be a part of the planet and not just an observer. If you leave the safe and sanitary illusions in the USA and go to other countries considered "third world," you can be sure you will be confronted with the reality of the masses. You will encounter great portions of the world's population who have not and will never rise above their plight.

Whether you decide to plan for travel wherein you spend a few days in many places or spend many, many days in one place, it is critical that you examine your attitude toward poverty and decide if you will be blind to it, repulsed by it or whether your life will be enhanced by the lessons we can learn from people who endure poverty and continue to love, smile, laugh and seem to be living life with joy.

There is much to learn, experience and see in your travels and whatever way you choose to wander is perfect and not nearly as important as that you get your passport one way or another and GET PACKING!

My personal passion is to travel to exotic places that sound interesting to me for one reason or another and then park myself for as long as my visa allows.

For me there are many, many benefits to this plan and I must thank God and my Uncle Sam for making it so easy for me to do this.

First of all, and if you are like most of us, there is a factor that is always a primary consideration. Money.

It is far cheaper to aim for a particular spot and settle in for 3 months or however long your visa allows, if you like it. More money will fly out of your pocket if keep moving all the time.

In most of the affordable countries you might like to visit it is possible to rent a house, an apartment or just a room with a family for much less than it would cost for hotels. And much, much less than it would cost for you to provide a dwelling for yourself in the USA.

The other great benefit of hanging out a while to get to know and love the locals is that the longer you plant yourself, the less money you will pay for a place to live. And you will get far finer digs. For example you can rent a quite cozy and maybe even glamorous house or apartment instead of staying in drab and tiny hotel room if you are willing to commit for a month or more. You'll have to scout around and ask a lot of questions, but in the end you will pay less than the hotel would have cost and have a far happier experience actually "living" in your country of choice.

Isn't this true in the USA as well? In the USA even a Motel 6 will cost you a great deal more than what you would pay to rent even a small apartment. However, in the USA it is very difficult to do this as you will be plagued with applications, deposits, first and last month, impossibly high rents, etc. So our minds don't tend to consider the possibility of handing someone $200 to $300 dollars and moving in that same day to a place that is fully ready for you to just bring your suitcase.

Nor is it likely in the USA that we would move into a charming place at any price that comes fully equipped with furniture, linens, dishes, pots and pans, TV and maybe even a fireplace.

I can only tell these possibilities exist because as I write these words in a village on Lake Atitlan in Guatemala I am living for just one month in just such a place.

I am sure I could stay longer and probably get a better rental rate or I could look around diligently and find, as a 75-year-old friend here has just found, an entire house with a beautiful garden, kitchen and bedroom. My friend intends to begin serving meals in his house in the next few weeks without the need for miles of red tape, permits and aggravation. His house will cost him $250 a month in rent. He will live there and never have to buy a meal out. And he will certainly NOT be wasting away watching TV and waiting for the grim reaper, which is something my daughter has told me she definitely doesn't want to see her own mother do. I am sure your children don't want to see you do that either. Ask them.

So how long is long enough? My recommendation is that you stay put for as long as possible and begin to feel like you are truly "living" in a place and not just an outsider. Anyway that's my idea of a good time.

FOURTEEN

Living NOW!

On September 28, 2007, when I made the decision to write this book, the title simply appeared instantly in my head. No other title ever surfaced and since that moment no other title has ever seemed possible. Indeed, because of the title, the book seems to have taken on a mind of its own, demanding that I, myself, never lose sight of the question, **If Not Now, When?**

This book is really not about travel. It is about life.

But what is life anyway? For me it is a joyous gift from God that we get to learn in and play in until we no longer have that particular gift of life available to us. We must always remember that the gift can be taken from us at any moment.

In the big picture, a single human life is a mere speck in the universe, the duration of which is less than a particle of a blip on the big screen of eternity.

Life is an amazing opportunity filled with possibilities. Yet, how is it that so many of us complain through so much of life and sleep through the rest – in and out of bed!

It's not that we don't want to hold onto life. We are desperate to keep it and we do innately understand its potential at the depth of our souls.

Suppose a killer walked up to you and said, "OK. Now I am going to end your life." It's a rare and unhappy bird who would say, "OK then. Whatever."

We are pretty clear that we want to live. Why then does our desire seem to fall apart when it comes to time? When we are wasting time, which doesn't actually exist (time that is does not actually exist), what we are in reality wasting is life – that precious something that we would kick and scream and fight like crazy if someone or something might threaten to take it away from us.

Again, this book is not about travel. It is about living. If you found it in the travel section, the book store staff simply didn't understand. In a perfect world they would have placed it in the section on "Life". Only I don't believe there is a section on "life". So they may have thought to put this book in the self-help or psychology or retirement planning sections or maybe philosophy.

Well. . . . . I myself don't really know where it belongs in the bookstore. I never have and what difference does it make. I know only one very simple fact.

If we are to live our lives to the fullest, we must do it NOW!

There are many wonderful, inspired and inspiring books that speak to living in the moment. I have read most of them and highly recommend them if you have time to wade through volumes of more justification to live in the moment than anyone should need to plow through to get to the point.

The point is simple:

THERE IS NO TIME TO WASTE!

You don't need to study up on theory. You only need to bump up against death a few times to be reminded how precious life is.

About two months after the idea and title for this book came into being, I sat in a hospital room with my dearest friend who I had known and loved since we both were fourteen years old. We were told she would not live through the day.

I prayed and meditated like I have never prayed and meditated before. Life became more real to me than I had ever dreamed it could.

Obviously there was no longer a reason to pray for life for her. So instead I prayed for my friend's safe and peaceful journey to wherever it is we go when we leave this life. There was nothing more for me to pray for because my friend was clearly going to leave her body on that very afternoon.

Of course, she didn't want to go. She fought for months and months to stay in her body, to be with her wonderful husband of almost 50 years. She wanted to forever be able to spend time with her children, her grandchildren and even her great grandchildren. She relished every graduation, every birthday party and anniversary. She lived for them. She fully enjoyed the cruises she regularly took and so often with many of her loving family members, sailing along with her.

I sat with my friend Sweet Caroline, her husband and daughters as she took her last breath. And I didn't need volumes of philosophical literature to tell me how precious and how very special life truly is.

When I look back over my friend's life and my friendship with her, I can journey all the way to our silly teenage years of giggling girl talk in buses on our way to high school every day for years. I can recall how we would lose our voices yelling at football games. I remember her wedding day and the joyous celebration as we danced away the night at a most wonderful Italian wedding reception. I can remember the beauty of her daughter's wedding. They both were married at the same wedding and I shall never forget how proud and beautiful my friend was that day.

I think of how my friend filled her life and her home with knick knacks and treasures, photographs of family and joyful vacations and so much love. So much love.

But my friend was not quite 65 the day she died. She never collected a single Social Security check. She never spent one minute as a retiree. She certainly had a life worth living and she made the most of every minute of it. But she didn't get to retire.

If you are reading this and are still healthy enough to wonder what your retirement will be like, wonder about this question:

If Not Now, When?

Being able to reach the age of 65 having maintained good health and the interest and motivation to have picked up a book like this – then you are being granted what you might say is a second chance.

Retirement, even if you have only a small income, is an opportunity to experience what may perhaps be, or at least has the potential to be, the most enjoyable, significant and yes, even fun chapter in your life.

Everybody doesn't make it to this special opportunity. So consider yourself among the lucky ones if you have the health to follow even some parts of this book and live at least some of your dreams.

As I wrote about previously, during the writing of this book I also lost my 41 year old son who struggled for years with bipolar disorder. There will be no retirement for my son.

Less than a month after my son passed away I lost another dear, dear friend who went to bed one night with many plans for his future but simply did not wake up the next morning. My friend was still a few years away from 65. He was so looking forward to leaving his job in a bureaucratic department of the State of California. There will be no retirement for that dear friend either.

If you are at all able physically and mentally able, and, if you have the least inclination to see the world, consider shedding your fears and attachments and reasons why you "can't" and seize your special treasure of life beyond 65 because it is a gift not granted to everyone.

The trick will be to not spend too awfully much time in pondering, plodding along and resisting. Think as fast as you can, act even faster and get out the door while you still have the health to get around and the time to live. And most important, to love the life you are living.

Do it now!

FIFTEEN

Affordable Spa Living

How about having a full range of benefits of a luxury hotel and a good night's sleep for under $8.00 per day? Not only that, how about spectacular views, perfect weather and amazing sunsets view from poolside.

Realistically, when we sign up to stay in a hotel we are asleep most of the time we are in those often extremely expensive rooms. You don't see the fancy bathroom and the glamorous swimming pool when your eyes are closed anyway. You aren't sweating in the gym or sipping your Cuba Libre by the pool while you are busy with all your sweet dreams. So what difference does it make where you bed is as long as it's clean, comfortable, warm, cozy, safe and quiet. Well, and a reasonable distance from a toilet.

So try this scam on for size and ask yourself if you still want to hang out in Anytown, U.S.A. forever.

This is a true example of possibilities from one lap of my research in Central America. I've just thrown this tasty little dessert in to whet your appetite for fun travel.

I asked around in the lakeside village where I was staying until I found a luxury hotel with a health club. For the extraordinary price of $25.00 for an entire month I have just become an official guest of the hotel with full spa privileges. This includes use of the beautiful health club that offers expansive views of the lake and volcanoes and use of the crystal clear, clean, blue swimming pool for lounging by and swimming in. It also includes use of the two Jacuzzis and the excellent sauna located in a glamorous dressing room with large, inviting showers fit for and even intended for rich guests.

Well, if we can figure out how to live like the rich and spend little money, maybe we are rich after all.

Having tracked down the perfect arrangement for my spa experience, I then set off to find a convenient place to sleep.

It may seem impossible but if we get our intentions into creating miracles for ourselves, they are just not that hard to manifest. (See the chapter on Attitude: Fear – or Is the Glass Half Full or Half Empty?)

After a bit of hunting, I rented a room in a very clean hotel right across the street from my spa hotel for just under $7.00 per night. The toilet is ten feet farther away than it was in my apartment in Sacramento but I can still walk a few extra feet, even in my old age. I might have paid even less than $7.00 for this room if I had been willing to haggle with the owner but when something works out to be as reasonable as $7.00 a night for a good, clean place to sleep, I personally am not inclined to take a few pennies out of the hands of the local residents. Haggling over hotel prices is, however, entirely possible, accepted and even expected in small, privately owned hotels in resort areas of many countries. This is especially possible in the countries that are affordable for the type of travel us retirees can work into our budgets. Also, since as retirees we may be more inclined to and are able to stay put for a longer period of time – a month or two for example – it is always possible to negotiate a lower price for a longer term stay.

It's true that for this kind of bargain price a bathroom inside your room is usually not standard. So it may be necessary to leave your room and walk to another room a few steps away. But don't most people use a toilet in a separate room a few steps from their bed – a room called a bathroom? It's really not that much of a challenge or inconvenience considering what I have in store for you after breakfast. If you must sleep in the nude, get a bathrobe. It's well worth it.

My nearly $7.00 room faces onto a lovely garden and it is near a number of restaurants where, in the morning, I can order eggs for peanuts. Not too far from my room, besides the toilet, is the shower. But why bother to use this modest shower at this modest hotel because, you will recall, for this adventure I am living the spa life.

Many people go on vacations to relax and hang out by a pool. In our younger years we were lucky to get a week of that kind of life and who ever really felt relaxed when it was time to head back to the office after a week? Usually we either were not finished relaxing or cried because it was so good we couldn't bear to leave. I've done that. At least now you have the time to enjoy this way of life for weeks if you choose. Even forever if you had a mind to.

At this particular moment in my research of fun living arrangements in third world countries, that's what I'm choosing to do – be a poolside slug for a couple of weeks. True my excuse is that it is part of my research for this book. How noble of me, huh? And also I personally hate shopping. So what's to do? Shopping bores me to tears, I can't really afford it on Social Security and besides, and maybe most important, I don't want to buy a bunch of things that I will just have to store or get rid of somewhere in my future as I already have had to do in my past! (See Homeless) I could go shopping for a bunch of gifts but haven't we decided that we have done enough already for everybody else and it is now OUR TIME? Why not totally pamper my tired old bones at a luxury spa which is not, as you might have guessed, offered at my $7 hotel?

So after I have my eggs, which I've just ordered for peanuts, I'm off to the spa to spend the better part of the day exercising, swimming, inhaling novels and travel books by the pool, relaxing in the Jacuzzis and/or the sauna and eventually enjoying the shower fit for the rich.

Personally, after all that exercise and my delightful shower I would enjoy a cocktail in the afternoon while watching the sun fall into a volcano on the other side of the beautiful lake. What I don't like (and can't afford if I want to keep living this deliriously delightful lifestyle) is the high priced cocktails served poolside at luxury hotels. Yet, here I am. I'm reclined on a chaise lounge with my feet up, reading a good book and wanting and deserving a cocktail to accompany my observations of the sunset.

I suppose there are a few reasons we might like to enjoy a cocktail when the day ends. One reason might be that we are drunks at heart and to that I can only say, to each his own. (see Bill W's Big Book.) Could be we think a cocktail looks good in our hand at a time like this. Just feels right. I'd go with that! Maybe we like the sound of the ice cubes tinkling in the glass. Or, it maybe we simply enjoy that slight little mellow feeling that a glass or wine or a screwdriver offers at the end of a glorious day in paradise.

The intention of this book is to put you in the mood to figure out what really pleases you. Having done that, our next task is to work with and around our dreams in a way that best enables us to enjoy extended world travel within a very limited budget for as long as we can possibly pull off this grand ambition.

So now it's time to ask yourself just how low you will stoop to enjoy your Golden Years, without, of course, breaking any laws.

A while back I bought a backpack for cruising around my village all day. I thought I should keep my hands free to beat off the street vendors and/or catch myself should I stumble on the beautiful cobblestone streets. This backpack happened to come complete with a pocket that insists be filled with a fair sized bottle of "something." When I bought the backpack it did not come with an instruction book indicating exactly what I must place in the pocket. Or if it did it was written in a foreign language. I imagine it was presumed that normally one would place a water bottle in that pocket.

Well, not being one to follow directions all that well, had there even been any, one day I wanted something with a little more spunk than water and I found a bottle of sugar free orange soda. It was very delicious and the label on it clearly indicated that the contents were "orange". When the soda was all gone I thought to myself, "Self, this bottle, now that it's empty, must still be good for something!"

It was at that moment that I decided that bottle would make a perfect decoy for homemade screwdrivers. Oh well. Why not?

In the USA, drinking in public is probably against the law. So of course few self-respecting good American senior citizens would ever consider walking down Mainstreet, USA with an open bottle of alcohol in plain sight. Even disguised as orange soda. I'm not sure why this is because I've been up to such frugal behaviors for ages with the only downside having been a headache later from having too much impecunious fun for a whole afternoon and evening.

But we are retired now, have been good kids for long enough and have, by God, earned the right to a little outrageous behavior in the name of having a good time – finally. Besides, there are not enough policemen in the countries where you can afford to live well on Social Security to even catch the bad guys. But we are not bad guys, are we? Forget local, say, Guatemalan cops, having any interest in grey-haired old Americans with vodka discreetly hidden in their OJ. They wouldn't track you down even if it were illegal to drink in public in those countries, which I sincerely doubt because it is only in America where we must be constantly watched and protected from ourselves all the time.

So go ahead. Fill your bottle of "Free Naranjada Con Soda" with some nice fresh OJ and vodka. And when you're all done swimming, reading, exercising, soaking in the Jacuzzi and showering and you are ready for a cocktail, enjoy a swig or more of your screwdrivers. Don't be shy. Do it right there by the pool, watching the sunset. After all you've paid your spa membership and only your conscience will prevent you from squeezing the most you possibly can from every moment of what's left of your life. And why not squeeze the most you possible can from every one of the few pennies you have to play with for the rest of your life as well.

Just learn to say "no thanks" to the poolside waiters and waitresses or order fruit juice or a coke. You need to think now first of yourself and save every penny you can to shine up your Golden Years. Saying no is a good thing because haven't you already said "yes" more than enough in your life? I know that's true because were it not, you would be rich right now like the people they built those fancy showers for in the dressing room of your spa. The people who even sleep at your spa hotel in those fancy rooms with their eyes closed - just as tightly as yours will be closed in your $7 room across the street. Only they will get to sleep by throwing away $70 or $120 or

232

$200. Or maybe even more. For one sleep – for one night. Let 'em! And whose dreams will be sweeter?

Variations on a theme called "frugal" might include: A lemon soda bottle recycled with white wine. A green tea iced tea works really great too for white wine. How about various berry flavored sodas refilled with red wine, recycled cola drinks spruced up with rum, etc. Or you can always keep it simple and just keep vodka or gin or white rum in your water bottle. When the waiter or waitress isn't paying any attention (which, as you have probably noticed is most of the time) you can spruce up an orange or tomato juice with a little contribution from your "water" bottle. This is a good plan because you can simply order the juice with ice cubes, do your own spiking and then, if it's the tinkling of the ice cubes that turns you on, you can have your cocktail, tinkling sounds and still have money left for breakfast the next morning. With this plan you can even have a hangover the next morning with your breakfast if you have a mind to have that much fun poolside, watching the sun set. I've done it. The quality of the hangover is every bit as potent as if you'd spent tons of money.

The adventure of transforming Old Age into Golden Years is all about using your imagination for living and drinking (if you choose) outside the box.

So get busy and invent more frugal ideas and share them with your cronies. And be sure to also give those cronies a copy of this book. Get 'em off the couch and away from the TV before it's too late.

I encourage you, within the law, to go ahead and do what makes you happy and doesn't cost a king's ransom.

At this point in life, we had best be relieved of a need to worry about appearances. Now is a perfect time to remember the old saying, "Pride cometh before the fall." Now is the perfect time to make your **own joy** your ultimate and primary goal. You've already given your all to everyone else for long enough. Your turn!

ABOUT THE AUTHOR

Since I haven't got a name to impress you and probably not a leg to stand on to explain why you should have read this book, I'll just have to tell more tall tales about me and how I got the wild idea to write up all this stuff. For what it's worth, here's stuff about the author.

So who am I and where the devil am I coming from anyway? What can I know? You've never heard of me before, right? So what can I know?

When the surprise of retirement hit me one day, a year or so before my uncle (Uncle Sam that is) would start to send me money (February 22, 2007 to be precise), it occurred to me that I wanted *to be* my dreams. Only trouble was I couldn't figure out how I would do that on a rather limited income, without having to continue working – which I surely did NOT want to do. Enough is enough! Besides, who has time for more drudgery at this point in life! Been there. Done that. Truer words were never spoken!

So I wracked my brain. Well, sad news. Brain wracking didn't work. I could tell it didn't work because I noticed that the brain wracking process failed to produce any answers and/or direction. I decided I needed a quiet place where I could just empty my mind and await an answer from the universe. Seemed a simple enough plan. And, as it turned out, a plan that did, finally, produce results.

This book is the result of the empty mind plan.

As I begin this book, I am sitting by a remote lake in Guatemala. I am in a tiny village at the foot of a few inactive volcanoes where I am surrounded by tropical vegetation of all types, shapes, colors and sizes. The sun is brilliant all around me as I wait in the shade of a huge banana tree for Tina, my charming German waitperson and new friend, to bring me the most spectacular breakfast.

As I sit on this fabulous patio restaurant overlooking the lake, I realize that the universe delivered my answer for how I can live my dreams on just the little money my uncle sends to me every third Wednesday of every single month – God willing for the rest of my life. The proof is that I'm here, writing to you, right now. And I'm living within my means quite comfortably.

The answer did not come as one might expect. It didn't echo from the heavens one day as a booming voice from a bearded guy hanging out in the clouds. And I was not to be blessed with direction from the universe without first struggling through a series of events that might, at first glance, have appeared to have been bad, unpleasant or at least unfortunate circumstances.

As I sit here enjoying the perks of paradise, it continues to occur to me that NOT sharing my process of figuring out how to live my dreams on Social Security would be criminal. I don't want to be a criminal, so to keep myself honest and out of jail I must carry on with this mission and hopefully you will find it enlightening or at least maybe entertaining.

In the little village where I'm living at the moment, called San Marcos de la Lago on the shores of Lake Atitlan in the Guatemalan highlands, there was, as of yesterday, only one business providing the use of computers and I'm too cheap to own a laptop at this point in my life.

Today is my lucky day because a second business is re-opening after suffering a technical melt down for several days following a couple of earthquakes and some massive wind-induced power failures. This friendly neighborhood internet café has agreed to give me a discount for just using the computer to write this book, if I promise not to use the internet.

So today is a very special day. Today I begin the actual production of this book, now a reality but heretofore only an idea whose time had not yet come.

It's January 16, 2008 (two days before my 66th birthday). I am diving into the writing of this book with the constant thought in my mind that it is my gift to others who are newly retired and maybe stuck right where I was 6 months ago – asking myself, "What now?"

Oh happy day. I'm retired.

On March 28, 2007 I pulled off my false eyelashes in my cubby in the lovely office of the largest real estate investment trust in the USA. I had been working for this fabulous company for almost three years. I handed my eyelashes over to one of my co-workers – a twenty something young mother in whose shoes I wouldn't have wanted to be for all the money in the world. She thought it was a gross move. I thought it was maybe the most fabulous and meaningful gesture of my life. I said goodbye to my friends and walked out of the best company I had ever worked for in all my 50 years "on the job". I was officially retired. Free.

Exactly one month before that wonderful day I had bought a package at a Sacramento tanning salon for 30 days of unlimited sessions. Yes, I'm sure it was not good for my skin. No one I ever told about my tanning project failed to share that news with me. Presuming perhaps that I hadn't given that a thought. But I didn't care. It was a kind of a statement of freedom. By the time I retired on March 28, 2007, I was so brown I looked like I had just returned from an extended vacation in the Bahamas.

During that same month I began, FINALLY, after 50 years at hard labor, to think about my future. A tad late you might say? The first thing I was sure I wanted to do was travel. To do that I knew I had to unbundled my life. *Lighten up* we might call it.

At the date of my retirement I was living in Sacramento but planned, for starters, to return to Southern California, where I was born and had lived for over 60 years.

At the prospect of retiring and living on Social Security, the value of a dollar suddenly took on a whole new meaning for me. While throughout my working years I had endless opportunities and high enough income to secure a financially sound and comfortable old age, I simply never did the things I should have done. Who knows why? Not me. And it doesn't matter one bit at this point since we have agreed to live in the moment and not in the past. Onward!

But suddenly, about a year prior to the time I knew my Social Security benefits would start, the reality of the errors in my judgment gave me a good smack in the face – a hard one!

To say I became tight, frugal and yes, a cheapskate would be a gross understatement.

As I pondered my move from Northern to Southern California, when my retirement date arrived, the first thing I decided to eliminate from the budget of my relocation project was a moving van. I'd had quite enough of those in my lifetime. I had relocated from Southern to Northern California in 2002 after my mother passed away. I had taken my then 17 year-old grandson with me and with some help at each end we had loaded and unloaded a rather large, rented, one-way moving van that we had filled to the brim with lots and lots of *stuff*. A lifetime's worth of things I didn't think I could live without. My attachments.

Between gas and the cost of the one-way van we arrived in Sacramento, way back in 2002, $500 to $600 poorer. By today's standards that was a very cheap move but we did use our own very young man power and grandmother power for the most part.

In contemplating my return to Southern California I decided to transform the thought of renting a moving van into an outdated and unnecessary concept. I saw the whole idea of a van as NOT in keeping with my new freedom. So I resolved to take with me into my retirement only what would fit my tired old 1996 Buick. A bit downsized from a huge moving van.

During the last month of my working life my daily mission consisted, in part, of eliminating all my unnecessary "junk" – much of which was all that stuff I had jammed into the moving van and declared just a few short years earlier, I could not live without.

"Unnecessary." Now there is an interesting word. Ponder that word and that concept as you read this book and you might be very surprised at how many different shades it might turn. Maybe we need a book. Fifty Shades of Unnecessary!

To further the elimination of my *unnecessary* stuff, I carefully made a list on my computer of all my significant possessions that seemed they might have value to me or anyone else.

To each item I designated a future home. For most items the task was quite simple. Friends and relatives were happy to become the new owners of things like my almost new exercise bicycle that just a year earlier I simply couldn't live without. That actually went to live with the recipient of my eyelashes on my last day at the office. Other typical household furnishings like furniture, dishes, my bed, etc., etc. were headed for new lives with other grateful new owners.

Within a couple of weeks I had eliminated enough of my "stuff" that I could comfortably hang out entirely in the living room/dining room of my beautiful apartment, with my bedroom becoming the triage area of my departing "stuff." I set up an air mattress in my living room where I still had a table for my computer and one other table for my TV. Most everything else had been hustled off to good homes.

I didn't want to waste anything so I took care to find appropriate homes for all my stuff. For example, I had a fatally broken sewing machine I had used as far back as 1964 to make baby clothes while pregnant with my now 43 year-old daughter. For that item I tracked down a Singer store and donated my machine so they could disassemble it and use the parts for repairs. The guy was very happy about that.

My hundreds of books that I had either already read or it appear I was never going to read, went to the library where I felt they would be put to better use than just filling heavy boxes for me to cart around.

During the process of divesting myself of what I had come to call my "anchors" I also spent endless hours on the internet examining, pricing and dreaming about all the places in the world I would like to see in this lifetime. Wasn't that an odd pastime for someone who in 50 years had failed to plan beyond what my Uncle Sam would drop into my checking account on the 3rd Wednesday of each month for the rest of my life? And, I must be very honest. I never gave a thought to even my uncle's plan either. It was entirely Uncle's idea to provide for my future as it seems I, myself, was clueless and certainly NOT on top of things in terms of my own retirement.

Still, I thought, "Why not dream? Maybe there will be a miracle somewhere along the way. I'm not dead yet. And, in fact, I'm very much alive and in perfect health. Dreaming can't hurt me. Unless, that is, I get too attached to my dreams."

On the wall next to my computer, which had become the center of my universe, I placed a very large map of the world and marked it with a heavy black line representing a dream trip that I couldn't afford. The path led all around the United States by train, followed by a plane to carry me from New York to London. Next, two months by Eurail through 17 countries in Europe. From Finland, an exciting trip from Helsinki to Bejing, China via Trans Siberian Railway. Then more trains or buses to Thailand and on to Singapore. From Singapore a flight to Jakarta, Indonesia, a train and bus to Bali and that was as far as the black tape on my map took me. All that travel, because it was mostly by land, amounted to only around $2,000 which consisted of lots of senior citizens discounts. The trip (only a dream anyway) ended in Bali because I learned I could stay in Bali forever by continuously leaving the country and returning every couple of months with a newly stamped passport and then applying for retirement status. My research told me I could live in Bali and even save some of my Social Security because, thanks to the terrorists, the tourists had become a bit disenchanted with that particular paradise. Maybe the black line ended there because I thought I would just like to stay in Bali forever or maybe I got exhausted from pricing pipe dreams.

But even if I could make that trip and settle in Bali, the question still remained, what would I do there 24 hours a day, 7 days a week? Watch the rice grow and marvel at the spectacular cremations that you can experience if you are really, really lucky and plan well.

Yet somehow having the map on the wall gave me a sense of freedom and endless possibilities. Even if I had no idea how to pull off my dreams, I decided I would keep dreaming anyway.

During that last month that I glued on my eyelashes every single day, I went to work every morning, and continued my process of letting go of my anchors, one anchor at a time. After work I would make my daily treks to the tanning salon. Whenever possible I would hand an anchor over to its new owner immediately. But some things, like clothes to continue going to the office, a few dishes, my computer etc., were simply scheduled for distribution at the very last minute – as I departed for my fabulous golden years on March 30, 2007.

When that glorious day arrived - when I was free to wander about the planet - I packed up my 1996 Buick with everything that would fit inside of it. Unfortunately I discovered, at the last minute, that everything would not fit. So I made a quick trip to UPS with three boxes of what later I decided I had stuffed with useless nonsense. Later I wondered why I had even bothered spending the money to send that nonsense. Truth is it's just very damned hard to let go of stuff.

At last, on the happy day of freedom, I cleaned my apartment as a responsible adult would of course do, in order to get her precious cleaning deposit back. With my bicycle happily hanging off the back of my car and just enough visibility to see big trucks, I took off joyfully headed south on California Interstate 5, headed for the beachside paradise of Ventura, California. I was on my way to the joys and freedoms of the retired life.

The feeling of knowing that everything I needed was in my car (and hanging off the back on a bicycle rack) was truly thrilling. I felt so free I cannot describe exactly what a relief it was to not be maneuvering a huge moving van and thinking about moving into an apartment. Curse the first and last rental payments, cleaning deposit, calling the electric, gas and cable companies, etc., etc. Not my plan.

I had lived in the Ventura/Santa Barbara area for over twenty years and heading there seemed to me like returning home after almost 6 years living in Sacramento - a nice place to live, with lots of trees and truly nice people, but hardly the garden spot of America.

Thinking always of trimming down my living necessities, I moved into a very lovely room in a dear friend's home with only a very minimum of belongings left to me, including my one piece of furniture - an air bed. Is an airbed actually considered furniture?

This beautiful home that I moved into is situated on a hillside overlooking avocado groves, in front of which are orange groves followed by more avocado groves and then the skyline of Oxnard. Finally, behind all that glorious view I could see the ocean and, on a clear day, fairly abundant in this neighborhood, I could see the Anacapa Islands. Spectacular!

What more could a retiree ask for?

To further elaborate on this glorious new life of perfect retirement bliss I must share with you the absolute freedom and leisure of my days.

I arose when I was good and ready. Which was almost always after the entire rest of my family had left for work and school. Sometimes instead of departing my wonderfully comfortable airbed I would just grab my remote control and switch on Good Morning America. I would enjoy that favorite program until Regis and what's-her-name showed up on ABC at 9 a.m.

There was no need to carefully apply makeup and eyelashes and curl my hairs. There was no manager waiting to see if I would arrive in the office on time, no more staring at a computer all day inside a cubicle where I would be living other people's lives and solving other people's problems. My time was completely and totally *MY OWN*.

Once ABC became dull I would enjoy a leisurely shower and a bit of breakfast, maybe in the sun on the patio overlooking that amazing view. Then I would check my emails and take my time sending long responses to friends. Seemed I had all the time in the world.

Later in the day I might wander off into the beautiful city of Ventura, which is nestled along the foothills that meander up the glorious Pacific Ocean to not so hard to take Santa Barbara. Every day I lived as indulgently as I pleased. Without spending too much money because, of course, I had become a retiree cheapskate. I discovered as many ways to live indulgently and at the same time frugally as a person could possibly manage to invent.

Some days I would sit in Barnes and Noble enjoying their vast selection of great books. Rarely, if ever did I buy the Barnes and Noble stuff. I would just read and enjoy delicious cup of Starbucks at the Barnes and Noble cafe. I always chose an Americano, which I immediately infuse with half and half. This concoction tastes exactly the same to me as Cappuccino and costs at least a dollar less. Why not? I never could quite understand why we would want to pay more for steamed milk when free half and half tastes better anyway. To say I am impecunious by this point in my life would be a gross understatement. I've become an expert at pinching pennies.

I would go off to visit my Vietnamese friends to have my acrylic nails tended to and several times a week I would, of course, make my requisite visit to the tanning salon.

True the nail thing was a luxury I could certainly have lived without - especially a cheapskate like myself who was allegedly planning to live on a fixed income. But for the tanning salon I discovered that buying lots of coupons worked out to be very, very reasonable and there was some wild idea I had that having a deep tan was somehow thumbing my nose at the world of working. In fact it was probably moving me closer and closer to melanoma. But the thumbing my nose at the world attitude was winning out. When people would comment on my tan and I would tell them of my frivolous trips to the tanning beds they never failed to tell me how bad that was for my skin. I was always amused that they didn't seem to think I already knew that and isn't it cute how everybody wants to save you. I somehow enjoyed reporting that I didn't give a damn about my tan or how bad it was for my skin because I had lived long enough anyway and had avoided the sun all my life, like a good girl. The bottom line was, now I plan to do exactly as I pleased.

Many days I would take my beautiful, nearly brand new, shiny red bike down to the beach and ride endlessly (well, back and forth anyway) along the lovely flat bike path with the ocean breezes in my face. I would stick the very excellent earphones of my CD player into my ears and listen to Michael Buble or Nora Jones crooning romantic songs into my brain for hours as I cruised along enjoying the surf and sand and ocean breezes. Sounds pretty fine, huh?

When I would get tired of riding I would sometimes stop at the most magnificent park on the beach and plunk myself down in the beach chair my co-workers at my last job had given me as a "bon voyage" present. I would pull from the little wine carrier my friend had also provided on my leaving work, my bottle of Two Buck Chuck Chardonnay, a Trader Joe's exclusive, and pour some into a real wine glass. Posh, huh? I would get all cozy in my bon voyage chair, open a good book and watch the sun as it set into the blue Pacific, while enjoying my hardly expensive wine for just long enough to be sure I could still drive home responsibly. Us oldies certainly cannot afford the expense of a 502.

Not bad duty so far, right?

It gets even better. The friends in whose home I lived are wonderful people. They are forty somethings and have child who at the time was around 7 years old. My friends are fun-loving, have lots and lots of their own friends coming to call all the time and there is always something delightful happening around their house. A most pleasant placed to hang out.

Everything about my living arrangement was purely perfect. I found all the very best restaurants with the most inexpensive possibilities. I've fallen in love with a delightful bar right on the beach that has drinks cheaper than any bar I've even been to and you can sit right on the beach with your feet in the hot sand and watch the sun set.

So what is wrong with this picture?

Absolutely nothing. But where is it going?

Where am I going? What about my dreams to see the world? What about those dreams I don't figure I can afford on a limited income but dreams that I also don't dare let out of my clutches lest I become depressed and begin to suspect that life is passing me by while I sit with a glass of cheap (but truly excellent) wine on the beach in my bon voyage chair. This has been a nice seaside interlude but when does my life start? I wiggle my toes in the sand and hope my life will start sometime before it's finished.

Back to the empty mind plan.

From March 28, 2007, the day I retired, until July, 2007 – in the wink of an eye, really – I discovered that I was clueless about what to do with the rest of my life. So I packed up again and truly did take off in pursuit of an empty mind.

I headed for an ashram in Northern California where the biggest feature of my agenda would be silent meditation at least three times a day. I had spent several weeks at this ashram a few years earlier in a work exchange program such as I described earlier in this book.

In this beautiful and spiritual setting the answers to my questions of what to do with the rest of my life actually did appear gradually over a few weeks. As I said before, the answers did not come from a bearded guy lurking about in the clouds. But still, I am convinced my answers were sent by a higher power and were sent because I had deliberately made myself open to receiving them and because I was, in fact, asking for answers.

The first flicker of direction came from one of the ladies in my program who was very well informed about the WWOOF organization mentioned earlier.

You can get WOOFF directories from all over the world but my friend only happened to have one for Hawaii. It was hard for me to believe that just one WOOFF directory, just for Hawaii, consisted of many pages of very small listings of many, many organic farms that offer living accommodations ranging from tent sites to private rooms. It was quite an enlightening experience to realize how much fun stuff was going on in the world that I had known nothing about.

There may be countless senior citizens who love to work in the dirt who might just be thrilled at the idea of spending their days working in the more laborious aspects of these farms. On the other hand, some people, myself included, might see themselves in a nice shady kitchen, chopping vegetables for dinner to feed the troops. That's also a pastime that's possible for many of these farms. But in reality the concept of work exchange on an organic farm is probably better suited to the young than it is to my peers. The concept however, of work exchange shifted my ideas about travel possibilities.

What WWOOF was for me was an awakening to the vastness of possibilities that I had no idea existed. It took my mind outside the box of commonly accepted activities and methods of travel and pressed me to explore the unknown in search of ways I might live my dreams of travel, despite my less than flush financial situation.

Branching off from the WWOOF concept I began to explore other websites that offer exchange programs. I discovered what my heretofore narrow mind would have missed in my lifetime. The revelation that the possibilities for affordable ways to experience the world are almost endless. Without paying a fortune for any number of directories of exchange programs I discovered everything from minding sheep in Australia to being a mother's helper in Spain, teaching English to the children and learning Spanish from one's students.

As I shared my travel plans and talked about my enthusiasm for work exchange with guests of the yoga retreat where I worked and other workers like myself, I would continuously be directed to interesting books like **Tales of a Female Nomad** and **Eat, Pray, Love**. Writings by women who, for one reason or another, took off on extended travel to learn more about life, discover themselves and experience the world.

The combination of thinking outside the box of commonly accepted travel methods, the wish that I myself would see the world on a shoestring and the idea of sharing possibilities with others, eventually led me to the desire to produce my own book.

As my mind was twisting and turning with how I would make my travel dreams come true, I was also dealing with a great sadness because my dear friend Carol (who I call Sweet Caroline), one of my beloveds to whom this book is dedicated, was in the last stages of a terminal illness and would be with us for only a short time longer. It became very clear that Carol would never see a single day of retirement. I felt she had been cheated out of something she deserved and worked so hard for. With this sadness blossomed the idea that retirement was, if we made it that far, a huge gift, filled with wonderful possibilities that we best not leave untapped.

The fact that so many people never live long enough to ever be challenged with the dilemma of what to do with their retirement became a matter of great significance to me. It left me so conscious of the fact that reaching the age of retirement and still being healthy is a treasure that the lucky ones among us *must* value. It was a gift we must not allow to simply fade away. I don't remember who said those famous words, "**Life** is what happens while you're making other plans." A Beattle, I think. Can we afford to be so cavalier about our precious gifts?

All things considered, the title, **If Not Now When?** popped into my brain and this book was conceived sometime around September of 2007 – before any of the people to whom this book is dedicated had passed away.

It would certainly be interesting if the publication of this book resulted in money in my pockets, which are quite famous for having huge holes in them. But money is the farthest thing from my intentions for the success of this project.

For me, the only success that can be realized from this book is that at least some of it's readers do whatever is needed to step out of a retirement that would not have manifested their travel dreams and step into a life filled with all the dreams, fun and adventure they still have the health and the time to manifest.

If some money should happen into my hands as a result of the publication of this book I'm afraid I will just go buy boxes of Spanish/English or whatever dictionaries and hand them out to the indigenous kids of whatever countries I can get to so some of us become better acquainted with our fellow humans before the world ends. "They" say that the Mayans say the world will end December, 2012. But "they" lie. I now – November, 2012 - live in Guatemala with the real Mayans and they say instead of reaching an ending, we will have a new beginning December of 2012. The Mayans say everybody misunderstood because it was only the calendar that was ending, not the world. A misunderstanding is all. Just in case, I'm getting it covered by pushing the "publish" button on Amazon so this book will be finally e-published before the end – or the beginning as the case may be – of the world.

If the rumors and misunderstanding win out and the world ends, then this book is the ultimate "moot point." If the Mayans have the true story (and since it's their story it ought to be that their story is true) that we will have a beginning rather than an ending, then I suggest you hurry up and GET PACKING!

After all, as I've said before, *If Not Now, When?*

30513410R00143

Made in the USA
Lexington, KY
06 March 2014